Second Edition

Guide to Intermediate Accounting Research

Shelby Collins, CPA
Accounting Research Solutions

Cambridge Business Publishers, LLC

Guide to Intermediate Accounting Research, Second Edition, by Shelby Collins. COPYRIGHT © 2020 by Cambridge Business Publishers, LLC. Published by Cambridge Business Publishers, LLC. Exclusive rights by Cambridge Business Publishers, LLC for manufacture and export.

ISBN: 978-1-61853-316-6

Printed in Canada

Foreword

For 16 years, I taught the graduate accounting policy and research class at the University of Georgia's J. M. Tull School of Accounting. And then, I worked closely with my successor to help him develop materials to teach the course. These experiences have taught me firsthand what a challenging, albeit rewarding, topic accounting research is for students, and what a challenging course it can be to develop. Prior to this position, my 26 years with Ernst & Young and 10 years as Chairman of the Financial Accounting Standards Board (FASB) have shown me that despite this challenge, research and communication skills are what set graduates apart in practice.

My class required students to prepare reports on real-world case studies and to participate actively in class discussions of research and current events. However, these research and communication skills did not always come naturally to students. I'll never forget the time when, after assigning students a case involving revenue recognition at CBS Sports, a student approached me and said that he could not find "NFL Football" anywhere in the accounting literature. I hinted to him that terms such as "revenue recognition" or "licensing fees" were more likely to result in relevant information for this particular case. Frequently, even identifying the right keywords to search can involve practice and finesse.

While the FASB Codification has done a lot to facilitate guidance searches, accounting research remains a daunting challenge for many students. In part that's simply because of the sheer volume of guidance included within U.S. GAAP, and in part it is because accounting policy issues often don't have black or white answers.

Shelby Collins is one of my former students, and a standout whom I had the privilege of nominating for a position at the FASB. When she approached me with the idea for her research textbook, I was immediately supportive. After all, throughout my 16 years of teaching, I was unable to find a resource that met the challenge of teaching accounting students the skills necessary to perform great research, let alone prepare instructors for the challenge of teaching this course.

This text does just that. Shelby and I worked closely on the initial draft of this material, and I am pleased to say that the result is a useful, and necessary resource that will enhance the quality of accounting research education—for students, instructors, and professional users alike.

With the help of this guide, we can make this challenging, yet important, skill more attainable for students.

Dennis R. Beresford
Executive in Residence, University of Georgia
Former Chairman of the Financial Accounting Standards Board

About the Author

Shelby Collins, CPA, loves accounting research. Her current consulting position, assisting companies with implementation of the new GAAP and IFRS lease and revenue accounting standards, brings a fresh and relevant perspective to this text. Prior to this position, Shelby taught the accounting research course at the University at Buffalo for six years. Her career has been dedicated entirely to this field: first at the Financial Accounting Standards Board (FASB) as a postgraduate technical assistant, then in KPMG's Accounting Advisory Services group, and then in the accounting policy and research group at Exelon Corporation in Chicago.

Shelby has seen firsthand the doors that can open for professionals who excel in research and communication. She is eager to bring practical, real-world insights to students in a way that promotes hands-on, active learning. Today, Shelby's text *Skills for Accounting Research* is in its fourth edition and fills an important need as accounting programs recognize the importance of offering a standalone research course. Offered by popular demand, this guide is now in its second edition and offers an introduction to professional research for intermediate accounting students.

Preface

Increasingly, accounting research and communication skills are being regarded as fundamental to success in our profession. Professionals who excel in these areas will likely experience a *distinct competitive advantage* relative to their peers. At the same time, in today's highly regulated business climate, the consequences of inadequately researching and documenting accounting judgments can be severe (e.g., PCAOB or SEC enforcement actions). Recognizing the importance of research skills, research simulations are now a key component of the national CPA exam. This hands-on guide aims to teach students these important skills.

In this guide, students will learn to confidently address and communicate accounting research issues, from start to finish. Students will not only take away the ability to identify the accounting problem (the "researchable question"), but will gain experience locating and applying guidance within the FASB Codification. In learning to use the Codification, students will have the opportunity to apply guidance to a variety of actual accounting topics.

Recognizing that students cannot learn to research simply by reading about research, this guide offers students numerous opportunities to actively apply what they have learned.

TARGET AUDIENCE

This guide is intended to serve a supplement to the materials used in an intermediate or advanced accounting course. It includes many opportunities to apply Codification guidance to related accounting topics (including, for example, leases, and revenue recognition). Practitioners and staff training programs can also benefit from the research and communication strategies covered in this guide, while gaining exposure to actual excerpts and topics covered in the Codification.

Colleges and universities are increasingly including accounting research as a curriculum requirement for undergraduate and/or graduate-level accounting students. Often, students reaching this stage of their accounting program will have just completed their first accounting internship. Interns, as with new staff accountants, will quickly discover that they are expected to learn on the job (accounting can be a sink-or-swim environment). This guide will provide students with exposure to research in a format that is understandable and engaging, allowing them to succeed in their future professional endeavors.

Prerequisites for Users of This Guide

To get the most value from this guide, students studying this material should have already taken introductory-level accounting courses. Users of this guide will need access to the FASB Codification research tool. The American Accounting Association (AAA) provides academic access to the FASB *Accounting Standards Codification* and the Governmental Accounting Standards Board's *GARS Online* database for a low annual fee of $250 per year, per institution.

OUTSTANDING FEATURES OF THIS GUIDE

This guide unites research techniques with actual technical accounting issues. Students will move their understanding of accounting issues and research techniques forward along the knowledge continuum, from simply *understanding* to having the ability to *critically think* about and *apply* accounting issues. The practical examples and exercises in this guide will challenge students to actively learn while they read.

Instructors will value that this guide allows students to independently read and practice the baseline skills necessary to become accounting researchers, leaving instructors free to expand lectures into discussions of accounting judgments, student presentations, current events, and classroom discussions of (or hands-on group practice with) case studies. In short, instructors will be able to actively engage students in classroom debates and discussions, because they can spend less of their valuable classroom time lecturing on basic research and communication skills.

Overview of the Guide

Chapter 1 provides an in-depth introduction to the FASB Codification, and emphasizes that students should perform *Browse* (as opposed to keyword searches) when possible.

Chapter 2 introduces the research process.

Chapter 3 introduces the fundamentals of effective technical writing, including the format of an accounting issues memorandum, techniques for effective email communication of research, and appropriate style for technical accounting writing.

Engaging Pedagogy

Research is a skill that you learn by doing; accordingly, the pedagogy in this guide is designed to foster active learning.

Chapter Opening Vignettes, Learning Objectives, and "Organization of This Chapter" Diagrams

Each chapter opens with a brief vignette placing students in the shoes of a beginning researcher. This opening vignette is followed by a list of the learning objectives for the chapter, and then by a diagram illustrating the organization of content within the chapter. These chapter-opening elements are intended to generate reader enthusiasm for chapter content, as well as provide students with an overview of the information to come.

Chapter Features

Chapters are written in concise, easy to understand language, with boldfaced key terms to call students' attention to certain topics. In addition, chapters include extensive screenshots from the Codification and diagrams illustrating key chapter concepts, intended to both engage students and improve their familiarity with research tools.

Chapters also include the following features, intended to engage students in active learning.

Now You Try

Now
YOU
Try

Throughout each chapter, students are challenged to practice and apply key skills as they are taught (**Now YOU Try** questions). These exercises might involve, for example, a student being asked to "draw a picture" of a transaction, "draft an email" describing an issue, "show the search path you would use," or "identify the journal entries" for a scenario, using guidance from the Codification as a guide for the appropriate accounting. Instructors can use these questions as a lead-in to active in-class discussions.

Tips from the Trenches

Periodically throughout the text, students will find **TIPS from the Trenches**, which offer additional insight on chapter content. These tips are designed to be like the insights you might hear an audit senior offer an audit staffer from across the table.

End of Chapter Questions and Case Studies

At the conclusion of each chapter, review questions and exercises are provided, which instructors may choose to assign as homework.

- The **review questions** encourage students to recall and apply key points from the reading. Instructors may choose to use these as a basis for quiz questions.

- The **exercises** provide students with an opportunity to practice their research skills using the FASB Codification.

In addition, **case study questions** are included at the end of each chapter, providing students with the opportunity to apply the research process to more involved accounting issues. Students may be asked to respond to these questions in the form of an email or by drafting an accounting issues memo. Cases of varying degrees of complexity are provided; accordingly, instructors may choose to assign case study questions as individual homework or as group research assignments.

NEW TO THIS EDITION

- New Standards: Includes strategies for navigating the revised revenue and lease topics and new assignments requiring students to research and interpret the new standards and to document and communicate their findings.

- Codification: Presents updated screenshots of the Codification featuring the latest standards.

- Updated Detailed Research Example: The author presents a real-world research question involving baseball stadium concession sales (Lease? Revenues?) and integrates it throughout Chapters 2 and 3. Students will follow this real-world example through the research, process culminating in a new chapter-end sample memo.

- Case Studies: The text includes new, current, and real-world case studies of varying difficulty level—including cases building upon the stadium example. Cases place increased emphasis upon the use of professional judgment.

SUPPLEMENTS

All supplements for this guide have been created by the guide's author.

PowerPoint Slides—Available for each chapter, PowerPoint lecture slides highlight key matter from each chapter.

Solutions Manual—Includes solutions to all end-of-chapter review questions, exercises, and case studies.

Now You Try Responses—Available to instructors, solutions to the **Now You Try** exercises are intended to assist instructors in leading class discussions.

ACKNOWLEDGEMENTS

I would like to first thank Denny Beresford, for his enthusiastic initial, and continuing, support of this guide.

We were fortunate to receive review comments on this guide from accounting research faculty from across the country, and we are sincerely grateful to these individuals for their time and important contributions to this guide. These individuals are

Sheila Ammons, *Austin Community College*
Marie Archambault, *Marshall University*
Salem Boumediene, *Montana State University*
Megan Burke, *Texas A&M University—Commerce*
Kimberly Charland, *Kansas State University*
Yu Chen, *Texas A&M International University*
Mary Christ, *University of Northern Iowa*
Ann Cohen, *SUNY—Buffalo*
Amanda Cromartie, *University of North Carolina—Greensboro*
John Crowley, *Castleton State College*
Abbie Daly, *University of Wisconsin—White Water*
John DeJoy, *Union Graduate College*
Victoria Dickinson, *University of Mississippi*
Lynn Dikolli, *University of North Carolina at Chapel Hill*
Tom Downen, *University of North Carolina—Wilmington*
Emily Doyle, *University of South Carolina*
Robert Elya, *Golden Gate University*
Patricia Fairfield, *Georgetown University*
Tim Firch, *California State University—Stanislaus*
Michael Fischer, *St. Bonaventure University*
Caroline Ford, *Baylor University*
James Fornaro, *SUNY at Old Westbury*
Jim Fuehrmeyer, *University of Notre Dame*
Carl Gabrini, *College of Coastal Georgia*
Catherine Gaharan, *Midwestern State University*
Patricia Galleta, *CUNY—College of Staten Island*
Alan Glazer, *Franklin & Marshall College*
Hubert Glover, *Drexel University*
Rita Grant, *Grand Valley State University*
Mahendra Gujarathi, *Bentley University*
Parveen Gupta , *Lehigh University*
Leslie Hodder, *Indiana University*
Patrick Hopkins, *Indiana University*
Ron Huefner, *SUNY—Buffalo*
Venkataraman Iyer, *University of North Carolina—Greensboro*
Mark Jackson, *University of Nevada—Reno*
Carol Jessup, *University of Illinois—Springfield*
John Jiang, *Michigan State University*
Vicki Jobst, *Benedictine University*

Jeff Jones, *Auburn University*
(Amanda) Bree Josefy, *Indiana University*
Ahmad Jumah, *University of Illinois—Springfield*
Sara Kern, *Gonzaga University*
Katherine Krawczyk, *North Carolina State University*
Sudha Krishnan, *California State University—Long Beach*
Benjamin Lansford, *Penn State University*
Siyi Li, *University of Illinois—Chicago*
Linda Lovata, *Southern Illinois University—Edwardsville*
Jason MacGregor, *Baylor University*
Dawn Massey, *Fairfield University*
Dawn McKinley, *Harper College*
Janet Mosebach, *University of Toledo*
Kelly Noe, *Stephen F. Austin State University*
Elizabeth Oliver, *Washington & Lee University*
Kevin Packard, *Brigham Young University—Idaho*
Susan Parker, *Santa Clara University*
Laurel Parrilli, *St. John Fisher College*
Terry Patton, *Midwestern State University*
Suzanne Perry, *Texas A & M University—Commerce*
Marlene Plumlee, *University of Utah*
Richard Price, *Utah State University*
K.K. Raman, *University of Texas, San Antonio*
Paul Recupero, *Newbury College*
Phil Rohrbach, *University of Richmond*
John Rossi, *Moravian College*
Beverly Rowe, *University of Houston Downtown*
Carol Sargent, *Middle Georgia State University*
Lee Schiffel, *Valparaiso University*
Barbara Scofield, *Washburn University*
Debra Sinclair, *University of South Florida*
Kevin Smith, *Utah Valley University*
Chad Stefaniak, *University of South Carolina*
Randall Stone, *East Central University*
Ronald Stunda, *Valdosta State University*
Walter Teets, *Gonzaga University*
Thomas Vogel, *Canisius College*
Robert Walsh, *University of Dallas*
Changjiang Wang, *Florida International University*
Christine Wayne, *Harper College*
Jeannie Welsh, *LaSalle University*

Jeff Wilks, *Brigham Young University*

John Williams, *Missouri State University*

Philip Woodlief, *Vanderbilt University*

Gail Wright, *York College of Pennsylvania*

Rong Yang, *Rochester Institute of Technology*

In particular, thanks to Sheila Ammons, Lynn Dikolli, Tim Firch, Jim Fornaro, Jim Fuehrmeyer, Richard Grueter, Carol Jessup, Sara Kern, Elizabeth Oliver, Debbie Sinclair, Nicholas Stell, Keith Stolzenburg, Jeff Wilks, and Phil Woodlief for their valuable feedback and counsel on the development of this text.

A sincere thanks to the many institutions that permitted the use of their material in this guide, especially the generosity of the Financial Accounting Foundation and the AICPA.

I would also like to thank George Werthman and Marnee Fieldman at Cambridge Business Publishers for their dedication to this guide.

Finally, thank you to the instructors, students, and firms using this guide. I look forward to your comments and suggestions.

Shelby Collins

Brief Table of Contents

x

Contents

Chapter 1

The FASB Codification: Introduction and Search Strategies

Jeremy has just been asked to research an issue related to his company's "volatility" assumption, one of the variables used to estimate the fair value of his company's outstanding stock compensation awards. Jeremy is a staff accountant, with only a limited understanding of stock compensation accounting. He doesn't feel very competent in this area.

Nevertheless, Jeremy gets right to work. First, he asks his supervisor for more background on the issue then reviews a memo describing how the company has estimated this assumption in the past. Next, Jeremy logs on to the FASB *Accounting Standards Codification* (the "Codification") and begins reading more about this assumption within the stock compensation topic. Before long, he has a basic understanding of the requirements for estimating volatility, and he is pleased to have learned something new in the process of researching this issue.

Continued

After reading this chapter and performing the exercises herein, you will be able to

1. **Describe** the purpose of the Codification, and the meaning of *authoritative*.

2. **Identify** standard setters that have contributed to the current body of authoritative guidance.

3. **Understand** the organization of guidance within the Codification.

4. **Perform** effective Browse searches within the Codification, reviewing all areas of *required reading*.

5. **Search** the Codification using other methods, including keyword searches, the Master Glossary, and the Cross Reference feature.

6. **Differentiate** between existing versus pending content, and understand how to interpret transition date guidance.

7. **Recognize** accounting alternative guidance available for private companies.

Learning Objectives

Continued from previous page

As you begin working with the Codification, your experience may be similar. You may be asked to research topics that you know very little about, and this may initially be uncomfortable; however, users of the Codification quickly learn that research is a skill you learn by doing.

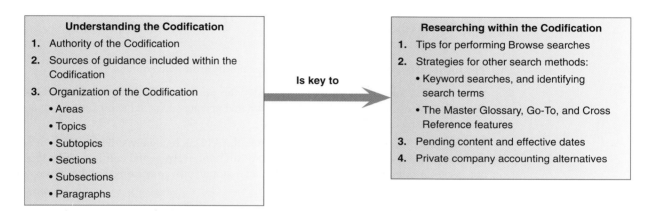

Organization of This Chapter

This chapter introduces the FASB Codification, including (1) the meaning of the term *authoritative*, (2) what sources of guidance were used to populate the Codification, and (3) how guidance is organized within the Codification. Examples abound in this chapter, as it is critical for beginning researchers to develop a hands-on feel for this important research tool.

Following this introduction, the chapter describes several methods for searching the Codification, including techniques for efficiently performing those searches. The chapter emphasizes that researchers should *Browse* to applicable research topics whenever possible, as this is the method used by research professionals. In our discussion of Browse searches, readers will learn not only how to find information, but also what other sources of *required reading* should be consulted to ensure that a research effort is thorough.

However, there are certainly times when keyword searches are valuable. The chapter describes how to perform such searches and offers readers the opportunity to practice identifying possible search terms. The chapter is rich in information, also covering other search strategies (e.g., the Master Glossary and Cross Reference feature), the role of pending content, and private company alternatives.

As illustrated in the preceding graphic, this chapter emphasizes that understanding how the Codification is organized is key to performing effective research.

WHAT IS THE FASB CODIFICATION?

LO1 **Describe** the purpose of the Codification, and the meaning of *authoritative*.

The FASB *Accounting Standards Codification* ("ASC" or the "Codification") is considered the primary source of **authoritative**, generally accepted accounting principles (GAAP) for nongovernmental entities. (Guidance from the SEC is also authoritative for public companies.) The Codification became effective in 2009, with the objective of simplifying research. Prior to the issuance of the Codification, accounting guidance in the form of individual standards had piled up for nearly a century. Accounting practitioners often had to search several different standards to find guidance on a single topic. This created the risk that practitioners could miss important sources when searching for guidance. The Codification reduces that risk by organizing accounting guidance by topic, within a single research source.

> What does it mean for the Codification's guidance to be *authoritative*? It means that the Codification establishes GAAP. In order to receive an unmodified (aka, unqualified) audit opinion, U.S. nongovernmental entities must prepare their financial statements in accordance with Codification guidance.

The FASB gets its authority to set GAAP primarily from two sources.

- First, the SEC, acting in its authority under the Securities Exchange Act and Sarbanes-Oxley, has identified the FASB as the designated private sector standard setter with authority to establish GAAP.[1]

- Second, in its Code of Professional Conduct, the AICPA recognizes the FASB as the organization with the authority to establish GAAP for nongovernmental entities. An auditor may not issue an unmodified opinion for financial statements containing a material departure from GAAP.[2, 3]

Using this authority, the FASB has designated the Codification as the sole source of its authoritative guidance.

The term **nongovernmental entities** encompasses both public and nonpublic (private) entities, as well as not-for-profit entities. However, these entities are not always treated as equals within the Codification. That is, due to resource constraints and often lesser demand for nonpublic entity financial statements, nonpublic entities are exempt from some requirements (such as segment reporting requirements) and are frequently given longer transition periods for adopting new guidance. The Private Company Council (PCC) was created in 2012 and advocates for simplified reporting options for private companies. The PCC's work has led to a growing number of private company alternatives available within the Codification.

Accounting guidance for *industries*, including *not-for-profit entities*, also falls within the Codification's authority. As industries often have unique activities and transactions, industry-specific content must be followed *in addition to* the other general requirements of the Codification. That said, in limited cases, industry-specific content may indicate that it should be applied in lieu of a specified topic or paragraphs from the Codification's general requirements. Industries addressed in the Codification include airlines, financial services, not-for-profit entities, real estate, and software.

---

[1] SEC Release No. 33-8221, *Policy Statement: Reaffirming the Status of the FASB as a Designated Private-Sector Standard Setter.* April 25, 2003.

[2] AICPA Code of Professional Conduct, ET 1.320.001 (*Accounting Principles Rule*), par. 01: "A *member* shall not (1) express an opinion or state affirmatively that the *financial statements* or other financial data of any entity are presented in conformity with [GAAP] or (2) state that he or she is not aware of any material modifications that should be made to such statements or data in order for them to be in conformity with [GAAP], if such statements or data contain any departure from an accounting principle promulgated by bodies designated by *Council* to establish such principles that has a material effect on the statements or data taken as a whole...."

[3] AICPA Code of Professional Conduct, Appendix A: "...the FASB...hereby is, designated by this *Council* as the body to establish accounting principles pursuant to the "Accounting Principles Rule...."

> Students are often confused by the role of industry guidance in the Codification. Remember: Industry guidance in the Codification generally applies *in addition to* other general Codification content.

TIP from the Trenches

Describe what types of entities the Codification applies to. Does it apply equally to these entities? Explain.

_____

_____

Now YOU Try 1.1

What Sources of Guidance Were Used to Populate the Codification?

The Codification is an aggregation of many, many accounting standards issued over the course of the past century. These include, for example,[4]

▨ FASB Statements and Interpretations,

▨ Emerging Issues Task Force (EITF) Abstracts, and

▨ AICPA Statements of Position.

LO2 Identify standard setters that have contributed to the current body of authoritative guidance.

Additionally, the Codification includes all still-effective guidance from the two standard-setting bodies that preceded the FASB, namely,

▨ The Committee on Accounting Procedure (CAP), which issued Accounting Research Bulletins (ARBs) and

▨ The Accounting Principles Board (APB), which issued APB Opinions.

In 2009, when the guidance from these original standards was moved into the Codification, the original standards were superseded and became *nonauthoritative*. Today, these so-called *pre-Codification standards* still serve a limited role in research.

Figure 1-1 depicts the many sources of guidance used to populate the Codification. All guidance in the Codification today has equal authority.

Key Standard Setters and Guidance Issued

Committee on Accounting Procedure (1939–1962)
– Issued _____

Accounting Principles Board (1962–1973)
– Issued APB _____ and related AICPA Accounting
 Interpretations (AIN)

Financial Accounting Standards Board (1973–present)
– Issued FASB _____ and _____, as well as Technical
 Bulletins, Staff Positions, and Staff Implementation Guides

Other Standard-Setting Bodies and Guidance Issued

– **Emerging Issues Task Force:** Issued EITF _____ and D-Topics

– **Derivatives Implementation Group:** Issued "DIG" issues

– **AICPA:** Issued _____, Practice Bulletins, plus certain
 content from Technical Inquiries and Audit & Accounting Guides

These original standards were _____ when the Codification became effective. All guidance in the Codification has _____ authority.

Figure 1-1

Sources of guidance used to populate the Codification

---

[4] To view the complete list of guidance used to populate the Codification as of its adoption in 2009, consult the FASB notice *About the Codification,* accessible from the homepage of the Codification.

Now YOU Try 1.2

1. Considering the discussion preceding Figure 1-1, fill in the blanks in Figure 1-1 with the types of guidance that were used to populate the Codification.

2. Then, in the blue box in Figure 1-1, fill in the blanks regarding the effects of these standards being moved into the Codification.

Additionally, the Codification includes certain content issued by the Securities and Exchange Commission (SEC), which is authoritative for public companies. Portions of the following SEC guidance have been included within the Codification:

- Regulation S-X (SX)
- Financial Reporting Releases (FRRs)/Accounting Series Releases (ASRs)
- Interpretive Releases (IRs)
- SEC Staff guidance in
  - Staff Accounting Bulletins (SABs)
  - EITF Topic D and SEC Staff Observer comments

However, it's important to understand that not all SEC content has been incorporated within the Codification. Some SEC rules and requirements, such as management's discussion and analysis (MD&A) disclosure requirements, are also authoritative for public companies but are only available at www.sec.gov, and in related accounting research databases.

The role of SEC guidance is further described in the following TIP from the Trenches.

TIP from the Trenches

> Students are often confused by the role of SEC guidance in the Codification. Here's what you need to know:
>
> - Guidance from the SEC *is authoritative for public companies.*
> - Portions—but not all—of the SEC's guidance have been included in the Codification. Companies can access the full population of SEC guidance at www.sec.gov.
> - Nonpublic companies may find it helpful, but are not required, to follow SEC guidance in the Codification.

How Is the Codification Updated?

The FASB is responsible for maintaining the Codification. As the FASB issues new accounting standards (referred to as **Accounting Standards Updates**), the FASB amends or adds to the content in the Codification. Accounting Standards Updates are not authoritative in their own right; rather, they serve only to update or amend Codification content. The Codification includes links to proposed and final Accounting Standards Updates; these are also available on the FASB's website (www.fasb.org).

NAVIGATING THE CODIFICATION

LO3 Understand the organization of guidance within the Codification.

In my time as an accounting research instructor, I've noticed a disconnect between how students are *inclined* to research versus the method that *professionals* use to research.

As a beginning researcher who has grown up on Google searches, your tendency may be to perform *keyword searches* in the Codification. By contrast, professional researchers tend to perform *Browse* searches, where the researcher directs the search by navigating to topics that might apply. In fact, the FASB actually *recommends* that researchers should primarily perform Browse searches, as well.[5]

Browse searches are a *user-directed* search. This means that you—as the researcher—would navigate to content in the Codification that you believe might apply. In doing so, you'll have *context* as you perform the search, and will better understand *relationships* between topics in the Codification. You'll also learn more about which paths *don't* work, often an equally important lesson. By contrast, **keyword searches** may dump you off into the middle of guidance that you may not understand, and that may not be relevant. These searches can result in some off-the-wall answers, trust me!

Figure 1-2 illustrates the difference between a Browse and keyword search for guidance on accounts receivable.

Figure 1-2

Browse versus keyword searches of the Codification

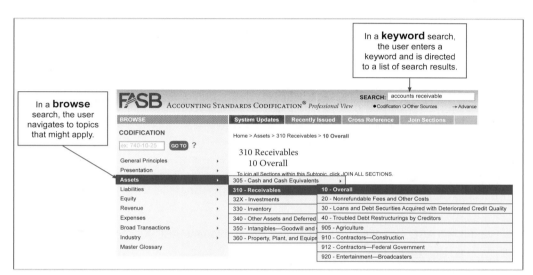

Reproduced with permission of the Financial Accounting Foundation.

A *key goal* of this chapter is to improve your confidence in performing Browse searches. In order to do this, though, you must first understand how the Codification is organized. To get the most out of this discussion, please log into the Codification and follow along while you read.

How is Information Organized Within the Codification?

The Codification is organized into areas, topics, subtopics, sections, subsections, and paragraphs. These categories are relevant not only to users browsing within the Codification, but also are used in *referencing* the Codification (such as in a memo). References to the Codification are generally presented using the following format:

Topic (XXX) – Subtopic (YY) – Section (ZZ) – Paragraph (PP)[6]

For example, ASC 842-20-30-1 refers to Topic 842 (Leases), Subtopic 20 (Lessee), Section 30 (Initial Measurement), Paragraph 1.

Figure 1-3 illustrates the location and purpose of these various categories within the Codification.

---

[5] FASB Accounting Standards Codification, *About the Codification (v4.10)*. December 2014. Page 6.

[6] Notice that areas and subsections aren't included in numerical Codification references.

Figure 1-3

Organization of content
in the Codification

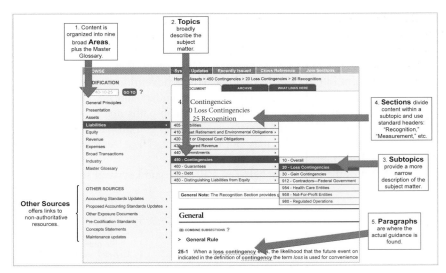

Reproduced with permission of the Financial Accounting Foundation.

Now
YOU
Try
1.3

1. Refer to Figure 1-3, then describe the following categories represented in this Codification search.

   Area: _____

   Topic: _____

   Subtopic: _____

   Section: _____

   Paragraph: _____

2. What is the ASC reference for this search? Use the format: ASC XXX-YY-ZZ-PP.

   _____

3. Now, notice the nonauthoritative "Other Sources" shown in Figure 1-3 . Name two of these resources.

   _____

Let's now take a closer look at each of these categories in the Codification.

Areas and Topics

The Codification includes nine broad **areas**, listed on the left-hand side, from which researchers can begin a Browse search. Within these areas, guidance is further organized by **topic**. Topics are generally titled in a way that indicates the subject matter they cover. For example, if you have a question related to inventory valuation, begin by locating the topic "Inventory."

Certain topics are organized into areas based on their balance sheet category. For example,

- The topic "Inventory" is available under the **Assets** area.
- The topic "Debt" is available under the **Liabilities** area.
- The subtopic "Treasury Stock" is available under the **Equity** area.

Straightforward, yes? However, where would you start a search for guidance on Leases? This topic is found under **Broad Transactions**. When you think about the different types of leases (e.g., operating/finance, and lessee or lessor positions), you may notice that leases are a unique type of transaction, and these activities do not fit neatly into a single area—Assets, Liabilities, or Expenses. Therefore, lease guidance is organized under a transaction-specific topic located in the Broad Transactions area of the Codification.

Where would you find guidance on employee pensions? This topic is found under **Expenses**. Costs related to paying employees are considered compensation expenses. Therefore, you would navigate to the Expenses area, then Compensation, to find the topic entitled "Compensation-Retirement Benefits." You'll find that locating the right starting point in the Codification requires a certain amount of trial and error. But after a fairly short period of experience, these starting points will become much more intuitive.

Here is a brief description of other Browse areas:

- The **General Principles** area includes information on broad conceptual matters.
  Example topic: Generally Accepted Accounting Principles

- The **Presentation** area includes topics related to how information is "presented" on the financial statements.
  Example topics: Balance Sheet, Income Statement, and Statement of Cash Flows

- The **Broad Transactions** area includes topics relating to specific transactions, or topics involving multiple financial statement accounts.
  Example topics: Business Combinations, Fair Value Measurement, and Derivatives

- The **Industry** area includes topics where the accounting is unique for an industry or type of activity.
  Example topics: Airlines, Software, and Real Estate

- Finally, the **Revenue** area includes the existing and revised models for revenue recognition, namely, Revenue Recognition (ASC 605) and Revenue from Contracts with Customers (ASC 606).

In particular, familiarize yourself with the list of topics located in the Broad Transactions area (see Figure 1-4). Topics listed under Broad Transactions are subject to specialized, transaction-specific guidance. It is inappropriate to apply general revenue recognition guidance, for example, to a transaction subject to transaction-specific accounting guidance.

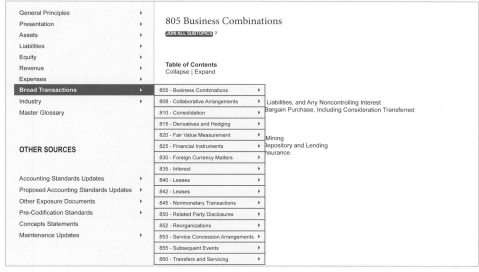

Figure 1-4

Topics available under the Broad Transactions area

Reproduced with permission of the Financial Accounting Foundation.

Consider the list of Broad Transactions topics shown in Figure 1-4 . Which of these topics, if any, have you had experience with, in your previous coursework or work experience? Put a check mark next to any such topics.

Now
YOU
Try
1.4

Finally, notice the link to access the "Master Glossary," shown on the left-hand side of Figure 1-4, immediately following the nine areas of the Codification. The Master Glossary is discussed later in this chapter.

Subtopics

Each topic is broken down into one or several **subtopics**. For example, the revised Leases topic (**ASC 842**) is broken down into subtopics including Overall ("**10**"), Lessee ("**20**"), Lessor ("**30**"), Sale and Leaseback Transactions ("**40**"), and so on. It is important to understand how these subtopics interact.

Each topic contains an "Overall" subtopic ("**10**"), which you should always make a point of reviewing in addition to more specific subtopics. The reasons for this are twofold: First, the Overall subtopic generally contains scope and other broad guidance that is pervasive to the topic. Second, the Overall subtopic can help point you to other applicable subtopics within the topic.

For example, even if you are performing lease research from the perspective of a lessee (addressed in the "Lessee" subtopic), you're still responsible for complying with any requirements and scope guidance available under the Overall subtopic as well.

In addition to the previously listed subtopics, certain industry-specific subtopics are available under Leases. Industry-specific content should be followed in addition to the other general content (unless stated otherwise). Assume that a "regulated entity" is the lessor in an arrangement. In this case, the researcher should check not only the "Regulated Operations" subtopic, but also "Lessor" and, of course, "Overall" for guidance related to that transaction.

<table>
<tr><td>

Now
YOU
Try
1.5

</td><td>

Identifying Subtopics to Review

Assume that you are accounting for a patent (an intangible asset) acquired in a business combination. You are trying to determine whether the intangible asset should be amortized.

Following is an excerpt of subtopics available under the Intangibles—Goodwill and Other topic (ASC 350).

- 10 - Overall
- 20 - Goodwill
- 30 - General Intangibles Other Than Goodwill
- 40 - Internal-Use Software
- 50 - Website Development Costs

1. Which two subtopics should you review in order to find potentially applicable guidance? For each response, explain why.

    _____

    _____

2. How would you write the numerical **ASC references** to these two subtopics (for example, ASC XXX-YY)?

    _____

</td></tr>
</table>

A final note: The subtopics listed in this example may describe accounting treatments that are unfamiliar to you (for example, "Internal-Use Software"). If a subtopic appears to be potentially relevant based on its title, read the Overview and Background of the subtopic to learn about common arrangements accounted for using this model.

Sections

Good news—guidance within the Codification is organized very logically, once you become familiar with the **sections**. Sections are used to organize guidance within each subtopic; each subtopic uses the same section titles, to the extent they apply.

Figure 1-5 illustrates a list of sections available under the subtopic Investments—Equity Method and Joint Ventures—Overall. Notice that each section includes a + sign, indicating that a user must click on the section title to be directed to content. Finally, notice that a user's search path is shown at the top of the screenshot. In this case, the search for the Investments topic began in the "Assets" area.

Home > Assets > 323 Investments—Equity Method and Joint Ventures > 10 Overall

323 Investments—Equity Method and Joint Ventures
10 Overall

To join all Sections within this Subtopic, click JOIN ALL SECTIONS.

JOIN ALL SECTIONS ?

Collapse | Expand

− 323 Investments—Equity Method and Joint Ventures
   − 10 Overall
      + 00 Status
      + 05 Overview and Background
      + 15 Scope and Scope Exceptions
      ■ 20 Glossary
      + 25 Recognition
      + 30 Initial Measurement
      + 35 Subsequent Measurement
      + 40 Derecognition
      + 45 Other Presentation Matters
      + 50 Disclosure
      + 55 Implementation Guidance and Illustrations
      + 60 Relationships
      + 65 Transition and Open Effective Date Information
      + 75 XBRL Elements
      + S00 Status
      + S45 Other Presentation Matters
      + S50 Disclosure
      + S55 Implementation Guidance and Illustrations
      + S99 SEC Materials

Reproduced with permission of the Financial Accounting Foundation.

So, how do you know which section is relevant to your search? Take a moment to understand what information is located within each section, as described below.

Section Number (xxx-yy-00)	Section Name	Description
00	Status	Provides references and links to Accounting Standards Updates that have changed the content of the subtopic.
05	Overview and Background	Provides general overview and background information for subtopics. Describes in general terms what transactions the subtopic is intended to address.
10	Objectives	States the high-level objectives of the subtopic.
15	Scope and Scope Exceptions	Answers the question: Does this guidance *apply* to my transaction? It is assumed that all transactions and entities are subject to guidance unless granted a scope exception.
20	Glossary	Defines all glossary terms used in a subtopic. The Codification also includes a Master Glossary, which includes all glossary terms used within the Codification.
25	Recognition	Describes *what* items can be recorded in the financial statements, *when* an item can be recorded, and *how* an item should be recorded.
30*	Initial Measurement	Describes at what value (i.e., how much?) a financial statement item should be initially recorded. Also known as "day 1" measurement.
35*	Subsequent Measurement	Provides guidance on how to change the value of an item after it is initially recorded. Also known as "day 2" measurement.
40	Derecognition	Describes when and how a recorded item should be removed from the financial statements.
45	Other Presentation Matters	Provides additional guidance on how the transaction should be presented in the financial statements.

Continued

Continued from previous page

Section Number (xxx-yy-00)	Section Name	Description
50	Disclosure	Provides disclosure requirements for a particular transaction or financial statement item.
55	Implementation Guidance and Illustrations	Includes (1) interpretive guidance describing how the guidance should be applied to specific scenarios and (2) illustrative examples.
60	Relationships	Provides references to other subtopics containing related guidance.
65	Transition and Open Effective Date Information	Provides transition guidance for content that has not yet become fully effective.
70	Grandfathered Guidance	Not generally relevant, but applies to practices that are no longer acceptable for new transactions but that some practitioners continue to apply to transactions that occurred prior to 2009 (when the Codification became effective).
75	XBRL Elements	Contains the XBRL-related elements for this subtopic. XBRL is a reporting format, for the benefit of financial statement users, in which companies "tag" certain financial statement data and information, allowing users to easily compile and compare information across companies.
S-00	"S" sections	Provides select SEC guidance, generally organized into sections similar to those described above. S-sections do not contain the full population of SEC guidance; limited guidance is provided for the convenience of Codification users.

* Note that the revised revenue topic (ASC 606) combines the Initial Measurement and Subsequent Measurement sections and refers to this combined section as *Section 32: Measurement.*

Certain of these sections warrant additional discussion. Following is additional background and tips for reviewing these key sections.

Overview and Background (-05)

The **Overview and Background** section provides users with general knowledge about a Codification topic and highlights types of transactions covered by the guidance. Read this section to obtain a basic understanding of guidance that is new to you.

Try to avoid citing the Overview as a source. For example, this section may say: "This topic introduces the requirement that . . ." Beware: Quoting this sentence is not as impactful as quoting the requirement itself. You would be better off finding the actual requirement in the guidance, for example under a Recognition or Measurement section.

Objectives (-10)

The **Objectives** section answers the question: What were the standard setters hoping to achieve when they created these requirements? Like the Overview section, "Objectives" should not be read as actual requirements; rather, this section provides users with overarching principles to consider when applying guidance requirements.

Scope (-15)

The **Scope** section is one of the most critical sections of an accounting topic. It indicates which transactions or entities are subject to guidance within the topic. However, beginning researchers often overlook this section, choosing instead to focus on the more "useful" guidance they expect to find under Recognition or Measurement. Pages and pages of professional literature have been devoted to analyzing nuances of the scope guidance contained within the Codification, as recognizing when you are within the scope of a standard is critical to properly applying the guidance.

Scope guidance is commonly presented in one of two ways:

- The guidance may list transactions that are *not* within scope. For example, scope guidance in **ASC 350-10** (Intangibles—Goodwill and Other) states

> **15-3** The guidance in the Intangibles—Goodwill and Other Topic does not apply to the following transactions and activities: a. The accounting at acquisition for goodwill acquired in a business combination. . .

- Alternatively, some scope guidance contains tests to determine what transactions should be included within the scope of the topic. For example, scope guidance in **ASC 842-10** (Leases) states

> **15-3** A contract is or contains a lease if the contract conveys the right to control the use of identified property, plant, or equipment (an identified asset) for a period of time in exchange for consideration.

To account for a transaction as a lease, a researcher would need to confirm that the contract involves 1) an identified asset and that 2) the contract conveys *control* over the asset.

Recognition (-25)

Guidance in the **Recognition** section describes what, when, and how an item should be recorded in the financial statements. Following are examples of each issue:

- *What* should be recorded? Asset retirement obligation (ARO) guidance tells you that the obligation to pay money upon retirement of an asset must be recognized in the financial statements (**ASC 410-20-25**).
- *When* should items be recorded? Revenue recognition guidance tells you when it is appropriate to recognize revenue in transactions with customers (**ASC 606-10-25**).
- *How* should items be recorded? Derivatives guidance states that derivatives should be recognized as assets or liabilities in the balance sheet (**ASC 815-10-25**).

Initial Measurement (-30)

Guidance in the **Initial Measurement** section describes at what value (or for how much?) a financial statement item should be recognized. This value is also known as an item's "day 1" measurement.
For example, in general,

- Inventory is initially measured at cost (**ASC 330-10-30**).
- Guarantee liabilities are initially measured at fair value (**ASC 460-10-30**).
- Property, plant, and equipment is initially measured at historical cost, including interest (**ASC 360-10-30**).

Subsequent Measurement (-35)

Guidance in the **Subsequent Measurement** section describes how to change the value of an item after it is initially recorded. This value is also known as an item's "day 2" measurement.
For example,

- Inventory obsolescence would be considered in determining its "day 2" value (**ASC 330-10-35**).
- Collectibility of an account receivable (for risk of uncollectible accounts) would be considered in determining its "day 2" value (**ASC 310-10-35**).

▦   Depreciation of property, plant, and equipment is considered in determining its "day 2" value (**ASC 360-10-35**).

Other Presentation Matters (-45)

The **Other Presentation Matters** section provides additional guidance on how a transaction should be presented in the financial statements. This goes beyond the presentation guidance provided under the Recognition section.

For example,

▦   Treasury Stock—Other Presentation Matters addresses where within the Equity section of the balance sheet to classify repurchased shares, when the repurchased shares may not be retired (**ASC 505-30-45**).

Disclosure (-50)

The **Disclosure** section sets forth required and recommended disclosures for a particular transaction or financial statement item. This section provides disclosures related only to the specific subtopic being addressed; other general disclosure requirements are addressed in Topic **235** (Notes to Financial Statements).

For example,

▦   The Inventory topic requires disclosure of "substantial and unusual losses" resulting from the subsequent measurement of inventory (**ASC 330-10-50**).

Implementation Guidance and Illustrations (-55)

The **Implementation Guidance and Illustrations** section includes the following, as applicable to each topic:

▦   Interpretive guidance describing how the guidance should be applied to specific scenarios.
▦   Examples illustrating application of the guidance.

For example, according to the Recognition guidance in the topic "Loss Contingencies," an estimated loss from a loss contingency must be accrued if the loss is probable and reasonably estimable (**ASC 450-20-25**). The Implementation Guidance section for loss contingencies:

▦   Identifies additional factors that should be considered in determining whether the "probable" threshold has been met (**ASC 450-20-55**).
▦   Illustrates appropriate accruals and disclosures for sample loss contingency cases.

SEC Sections (S-00)

SEC sections are identified in the Codification by an "S" that precedes the section reference number. These sections include accounting and reporting guidance that is authoritative for public companies. Often, SEC guidance offers further interpretation of general Codification requirements; for this reason, although the guidance is only required for public companies, public and nonpublic companies alike can benefit from the SEC's interpretations of GAAP.

SEC guidance is generally organized into the same sections as other Codification content. For example, **S-25** offers SEC recognition guidance. However, beware: Creators of the Codification did not want to change content issued by the SEC; therefore, any content not fitting neatly within separate sections (e.g., **S-25** for recognition) is available under **S-99**. Therefore, researchers searching for recognition guidance should check both sections: **S-25** and **S-99**.

The following **Now YOU Try** is intended to improve your familiarity with *sections* in the Codification.

Understanding Sections

Now
YOU
Try
1.6

For this example, we'll use a sample of the guidance from possibly one of the most daunting topics in the Codification—Derivatives (**ASC 815**). Your challenge will be to label each excerpt from the Derivatives topic with the **section** in which the excerpt is located. Then, identify the likely **paragraph number** for this excerpt (presented as Section XX – Paragraph YY).

As you'll notice in this example, the guidance within a topic becomes much more approachable once you understand how it is organized.

Sections to select from: Scope, Recognition, Initial Measurement, Subsequent Measurement, Other Presentation Matters, Disclosure, or Implementation Guidance.
Paragraphs to select from (from ASC 815-10): par. **15-83**, **25-1**, **30-1**, **35-1** and **35-2**, **45-4**, **50-1**, **55-1**.

		Section?	Likely Para. Number?
1	An entity shall recognize all of its derivative instruments in its statement of financial position as either assets or liabilities depending on the rights or obligations under the contracts.	_____	_____
2	Definition of a derivative instrument A derivative instrument is a financial instrument or other contract with all of the following characteristics. . . .	_____	_____
3	An entity with derivative instruments . . . shall disclose information to enable users of the financial statements to understand all of the following: a. How and why an entity uses derivative instruments (or such nonderivative instruments) . . .	_____	_____
4	This section provides guidance on the following implementation matters: a. Determining whether a contract is within the scope of this Subtopic b. Unit of accounting—a transferable option is considered freestanding, not embedded c. Definition of derivative instrument d. Instruments not within scope . . .	_____	_____
5	All derivative instruments shall be measured initially at fair value.	_____	_____
6	All derivative instruments shall be measured subsequently at fair value.	_____	_____
7	Unless the conditions in paragraph 210-20-45-1 [Balance Sheet > Offsetting] are met, the fair value of derivative instruments in a loss position shall not be offset against the fair value of derivative instruments in a gain position.	_____	_____

Subsections and Paragraphs

Paragraphs are where the actual guidance is found within the Codification. Paragraphs are sometimes organized into groups, called **subsections**. For example, within the Receivables topic (**ASC 310-10**), guidance is organized into a General subsection and a subsection for Acquisition, Development, and Construction Arrangements. Each of these subsections has unique scope and recognition guidance. Whenever you find a paragraph with content that appears relevant to your search, be certain that you understand the context. That is, be sure you are reading guidance within a subsection that is relevant to your issue.

For example, assume you word search (ctrl + f) within the Receivables topic for "residual profit" and land in section "a" (bolded below).

> **Assets > Receivables > Overall > Recognition**
>
> **General**
>
> a. Factoring arrangements
> b. Loan syndications and loan participations
> c. Standby commitments
> d. . . .
>
> **Acquisition, Development, and Construction Arrangements**
>
> **a. Expected residual profit**
> b. Characteristics implying investment in real estate or joint ventures
> c. . . .

Before you share this paragraph with your supervisor, wait! Consider the context. Did you intend to search within this specific subsection of guidance? Is your transaction within the scope of this subsection? To avoid errors, be sure to scroll up and down on the page to understand all related section and subsection headers when you find guidance that appears to be on point.

In addition to understanding what subsection you are in within the guidance, you must also pay attention to *paragraph groups*, indicated by a header and **>>** notations. For example, paragraphs could be organized as follows:

Issue header
>Issue 1
>>Subissue A
>>Subissue B
>Issue 2

Assume that you encounter paragraphs organized in this fashion, and the guidance in Subissue B is relevant to your research. Since Subissues A and B are extensions of the guidance in Issue 1, it would not be appropriate to follow the guidance in Subissue B without also reading Issue 1. You would not be required to read Subissue A if it does not appear to be applicable.

Now
YOU
Try
1.7

Subsections and Paragraphs

Following is an example from **ASC 820** (Fair Value Measurement), showing the organization of certain paragraphs within the Subsequent Measurement section.
> Definition of Fair Value

>>   The Asset or Liability
>>   The Transaction
>>   Market Participants
>>   The Price
>>   Application to Nonfinancial Assets

>>>   **Highest and Best Use for Nonfinancial Assets**
>>>   Valuation Premise for Nonfinancial Assets

>>   Application to Liabilities and Instruments Classified in a Reporting Entity's Shareholders' Equity

Questions:

1. If you find guidance you are looking for under the header "Highest and Best Use for Nonfinancial Assets," what two other issues should you also read?

    _____

    _____

(continued)

Continued from previous page

2. Explain.

_____

_____

If you lose track of where you are in the Codification, you can hover your mouse over the paragraph number to be reminded of the subtopic and section number for your current location.

For example, by hovering your mouse over par. 15-6 (circled in the illustration), you'll see the "Currently Viewing" screen, which describes your location.

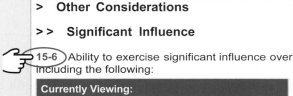

> **Other Considerations**

> > **Significant Influence**

15-6 Ability to exercise significant influence over including the following:

Currently Viewing:

323 Investments—Equity Method and Joint Ventures
   10 Overall
      15 Scope and Scope Exceptions
      General
         > Other Considerations
            >> Significant Influence

Reproduced with permission of the Financial Accounting Foundation (circle and cursor image added).

Let's look now at some tips for performing effective, and efficient, Browse searches.

TIPS FOR PERFORMING BROWSE SEARCHES

Now that you have a basic understanding of how the Codification is organized, you are capable of performing basic searches using the **Browse** feature.

As noted previously, the Browse feature is essentially a user-directed search. You, as the user, will click through a series of topics and subtopics that will, with a little experience, take you right to the appropriate guidance for a given transaction. As your understanding of the Codification increases, your efficiency in performing these searches will improve.

The starting point in a Browse search is to locate the specific topic and subtopic that you are searching for. See Figure 1-6, illustrating a researcher browsing to the subtopic Revenue from Contracts with Customers—Overall (**ASC 606-10**).

LO4 Perform effective Browse searches within the Codification, reviewing all areas of *required reading*.

Join All Sections

Once you're in the appropriate subtopic, I suggest that you click on the **Join All Sections** button. This button displays all subtopic content on one page and allows you to navigate more easily through the subtopic.

Figure 1-6

Example of a Browse search

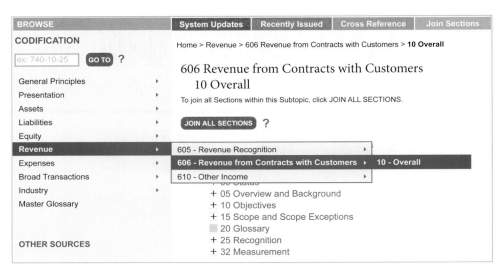

Reproduced with permission of the Financial Accounting Foundation.

For example, assume you are looking for the term *collectibility*, and you know the term is somewhere within this revenue subtopic (ASC 606-10). Selecting "Join All Sections" puts the full content of the subtopic on one page, allowing you to search the full subtopic for this term using "ctrl + F" (find).

Navigating a Subtopic, Considering All Areas of "Required Reading"

You are now ready to begin reviewing the subtopic for relevant guidance. As discussed earlier in this chapter, the first section you should read, if you are unfamiliar with a subtopic, is the Overview section (**05**). Next, consult the Scope section (**15**) to confirm that your specific transaction is within the scope of this guidance. Then, think about what question you are asking: Is it about Recognition? Initial Measurement?

Go to the appropriate section, and find guidance applicable to your search question. Let's assume that relevant guidance was available in par. 1 under Recognition. You've found your answer; you're done, right? Not so fast.

There are several important additional steps that you should "check off" before you can be confident that your research effort was thorough. In particular, treat any relevant Implementation Guidance and SEC content (particularly for public companies) as required reading. Often, the interpretive guidance located in these sections can confirm or change your view of how the guidance should be applied. Also, remember that these sections are equally as authoritative as other sections within the topic.

Figure 1-7 illustrates the following steps:

1. Confirm that your transaction (or entity) is within scope.

2. Look for guidance in the section that you anticipate is most relevant. For example, after confirming that your transaction is within the scope of a topic, head straight to "Recognition" for questions about recognizing an asset.

3. Ensure that you have read any preceding paragraphs that are related. In doing so, pay attention to the hierarchy of paragraphs, indicated by > >.

4. Fully skim the rest of the section you are searching (for example, the full Recognition section), to ensure that you have considered all relevant guidance. Subsequent paragraphs within that section may offer additional detail or situation-specific guidance that you should consider. Pay particular attention to boldfaced headings used to organize paragraphs, as they can assist you in quickly determining whether groups of paragraphs are potentially relevant.

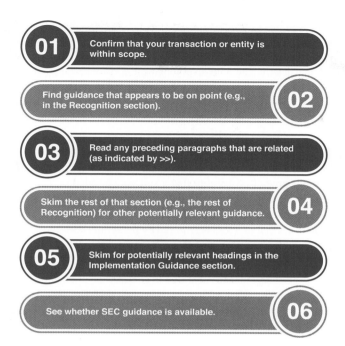

Figure 1-7

A checklist of required reading

5. Review the list of issues addressed within the Implementation Guidance section (**55**). In some cases, the first paragraph of the Implementation Guidance section includes a list of issues it addresses; in other cases, you may have to skim through the guidance, reviewing for potentially relevant headings (e.g., headings related to Recognition).

6. Particularly for public companies, scan the S-sections to check for relevant SEC guidance. Look in particular for guidance related to the section you are searching (e.g., S-25 and S-99 may both offer recognition guidance).

Be patient; it may initially be frustrating to use the Browse feature as your primary means for searching the Codification. However, it is essential that you learn how the guidance is organized. You will become more efficient with practice.

The following example illustrates how Implementation Guidance can assist in interpreting content within the Codification.

EXAMPLE ——

Understanding Why Implementation Guidance (Section 55) Is Integral to Your Browse Search

Assume that a customer slipped and fell in ABC Grocery, but the customer has *not yet filed suit*. Should ABC Grocery record a loss, due to the possibility that the customer will file a lawsuit? If the customer does file suit, the amount of loss is expected to be approximately $100,000.

ASC 450-20 (Loss Contingencies) states:

> **25-2** An estimated loss from a loss contingency shall be accrued by a charge to income if both of the following conditions are met:
>   a. Information available before the financial statements are issued or are available to be issued . . . indicates that it is probable that an asset had been impaired or a liability had been incurred at the date of the financial statements . . .
>   b. The amount of loss can be reasonably estimated.

Continued

Continued from previous page

> The preceding guidance states that a loss should be recorded if it is *probable* that a liability has been incurred; this determination involves judgment. Experienced researchers know that additional guidance, when available, can assist in framing judgmental issues. After finding this guidance under Recognition, look for Recognition guidance in the Implementation Guidance section (**55**). There, you can find the following guidance even more specific to this issue:
>
> > Assessing Probability of the Incurrence of a Loss (**ASC 450-20**)
> > **55-14** With respect to *unasserted claims and assessments*, an entity must determine the degree of probability that a suit may be filed or a claim or assessment may be asserted and the possibility of an unfavorable outcome. If an unfavorable outcome is probable and the amount of loss can be reasonably estimated, accrual of a loss is required by paragraph **450-20-25-2**. [Italicized emphasis added].
>
> Armed with this guidance, management should consider the probability that a suit will be filed, as well as the probability of an unfavorable outcome. Both guidance references (par. **25-2** and par. **55-14**) should be cited in a memo documenting the position taken. Note: Even if no accrual is made, it is a best practice to document the basis for such a judgment.

Next, let's look at an example illustrating how—particularly for public companies—reviewing SEC content is critical to carefully researching an issue.

EXAMPLE

> ### Understanding Why SEC Content (Section "S") Can Be Integral to Your Browse Search
>
> A public company applying **ASC 480-10** (Distinguishing Liabilities from Equity) will report equity instruments with certain redemption features differently than would a private company following the FASB's guidance alone:
>
> - A private company applying the guidance in **ASC 480-10-25** would conclude that equity instruments with certain redemption features should be classified as equity.
> - A public company would also be required to consult **ASC 480-10-S99**. In doing so, the public company might conclude that equity instruments with these same redemption features should be classified as "temporary equity" (a separate category).
>
> A public company's research would be lacking if it did not include consideration of both sources of literature just shown.
>
> Notice how the preceding SEC guidance came from Section **S-99**? As noted previously, SEC content not clearly fitting within a single section (such as **S-25** for recognition) is available under **S-99**. A researcher in this case should check for SEC recognition guidance in both Sections: **S-25** and **S-99**.

Now
YOU
Try
1.8

1. Describe how, in the preceding contingent liability example, the Implementation Guidance (Section **55**) goes beyond the Recognition guidance (Section **25**).

   _____

   _____

2. Which companies are required to consult guidance in the "S" sections? Explain.

Continued

Continued from previous page

OTHER SEARCH METHODS

In addition to Browse searches, several other methods are available for searching the Codification:

> **LO5** **Search** the Codification using other methods, including keyword searches, the Master Glossary, and the Cross Reference feature.

1. Search by **keyword**, using the Search/Advanced Search feature.

2. Jump directly to guidance using the **ASC reference number** (e.g., type in **ASC 820-10-30-1** to jump directly to fair value measurement guidance).

3. **Cross-reference** by the "historical" GAAP designation (e.g., type in **FAS 157** to be directed to **ASC 820**).

4. Search using the **Master Glossary**, finding a keyword of interest and clicking on that word to be directed to the guidance.

> These search methods are discussed further in the sections that follow.

Keyword Searches

A **keyword search** (i.e., a text search) is most useful when you are looking for a specific term in the guidance, or when you are uncertain where you would begin a browse search. For example, assume you want to find guidance on "involuntary conversions." Unless you have experience with this topic, you would likely not know that this term is addressed primarily in **ASC 610-30** (Other Income—Gains and Losses on Involuntary Conversions). In this case, a keyword search would be appropriate.

When a researcher performs a keyword search, the results of the search are listed by topic and include an excerpt from the guidance containing the term. As this type of search allows researchers to see a term in multiple contexts, keyword searches can be a useful brainstorming tool. Researchers can choose to pursue one or several search results, or the results can be used to generate ideas for other search terms that might be effective.

Figure 1-8 illustrates a simple search for the term "involuntary conversion" (see search bar at top right). Notice that sixteen search results were found, in areas including Revenue, Liabilities, and Broad Transactions. Researchers seeking to narrow instances of this term to a single area (or multiple areas)—or by related term—can use the "Narrow" option shown on the right-hand side of Figure 1-8.

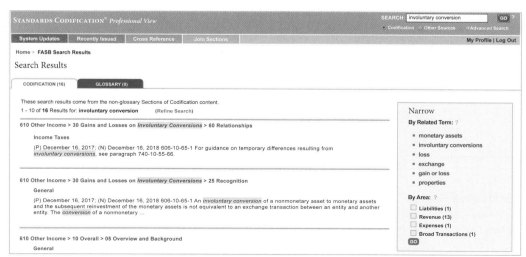

Figure 1-8

Search results for the term "involuntary conversion"

Users can choose to conduct either simple or advanced searches. A simple search involves a simple empty search bar, similar to Google. This is the type of search illustrated in Figure 1-8. Note the following about the simple keyword search:[7]

- Multiple terms: Entering **debt restructuring** is equivalent to searching for **debt** and **restructuring**.
- Phrases: To search for an exact phrase, use quotes. For example, entering **"major maintenance"** returns results about **Planned Major Maintenance Activities**.
- Singular/plural: A search for either **intangible** or **intangibles** will yield the same results.
- Wildcard (*): Add an asterisk (*) to the end of a word to find all forms of the word. Example: Deposit* will return **deposit**, **deposited**, **depositor**, **depository**, and so on.

An advanced search offers additional search options. For example, users can enter a phrase, such as **involuntary conversion** and can elect to search for

- "any" words (results will display any guidance containing the word **involuntary** OR **conversion**),
- "all" (results will display any guidance containing both **involuntary** AND **conversion**),
- "exact phrase," or
- words that occur within "n" words of each other (for example, users can specify that **involuntary** and **conversion** must be within five words of each other).

The advanced search feature also allows users to choose a specific area to search; for example, a user could specify upfront that search results for **involuntary conversion** must be from the Revenue area. Figure 1-9 illustrates an advanced search for the exact phrase **involuntary conversion**, limited by area.

Figure 1-9

Advanced search for an exact phrase, limited by area

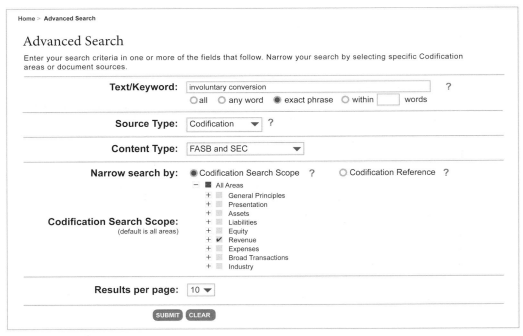

Reproduced with permission of the Financial Accounting Foundation.

Identifying Search Terms

Keyword searches are based on specific language. Therefore, you must use proper **search terms** (terms that are actually found in the guidance), or you will not find the appropriate guidance.

---

[7] Source: FASB Codification, Search Help.

Identifying search terms can be a sort of brainstorming exercise. Write down all possible terms that you think might be useful, including words that may be synonymous with other search terms you have identified. With time, you'll learn the terms used most commonly in the accounting literature.

After entering a search term, a researcher will be directed to a search results page. At this point, a researcher can choose to pursue one or several search results, or the researcher could use the results to generate ideas for other search terms that might be effective.

Following are steps a researcher can take to determine whether a result he or she has pursued is relevant (and if not, what to do):

1. If you see a paragraph in the search results that appears to be directly on point, follow your instinct! Read that paragraph and determine whether it is responsive to your question.

2. If, however, the search results just lead you to a topic but no perfect paragraph, begin by reviewing the Overview and Background section of that topic. See whether the guidance appears to be on the right track for your search.

3. Next, review the scope section for the topic. Is your issue within the scope of this guidance?

4. As you perform the preceding steps, take note of other useful terms, or links to other related guidance. Perhaps these clues will lead to more relevant guidance, if what you're reading is not already on point.

5. Finally, if you have hit a "dead-end" (the guidance doesn't appear to apply, and you have not successfully identified alternate search terms), scroll down to Section **60** of that topic (Relationships). This section includes links to other related topics; reviewing this list might trigger ideas, as well.

Following are two examples illustrating the brainstorming exercise involved in identifying search terms. Note that a "researchable question" has been identified for each situation below. Researchable questions are discussed further in Chapter 2.

EXAMPLE ───

Situation 1:

Company A (your company) has acquired 51% of the common stock of Company B.
- Researchable question: How should Company A account for its investment in Company B?
- Possible search terms: equity investment, acquisition, investment, equity method, consolidation, consolidate, majority owner

Commentary—Situation 1:

Very little information is given about this situation; additional facts would be needed before an accounting position could be selected. That said, we have sufficient information to brainstorm some possible initial searches.

Unfortunately, beginning researchers often have to learn through trial and error which search paths are most effective for a given situation. For example, guidance on *whether* to consolidate an investee is located under the topic "Consolidation" (under the "Broad Transactions" area). A search for the term "acquisition," on the other hand, will generally land you in business combinations guidance, which describes *how* to consolidate a majority-owned subsidiary. In this case, therefore, a search for "consolidation" would be more effective than guidance on "acquisitions," since you need to decide whether consolidation is required.

A search for the terms "majority" or "majority owner" is likely to lead a researcher to click on the Consolidation topic, so these terms would be effective. However, a search for the term "equity investment" or "equity method" will land researchers in guidance that does not apply, given that this situation involves a purchase of greater than 50% of the outstanding common shares of an entity. Reviewing the Overview or the Scope guidance in these topics will indicate to the researcher that another search term should be tried.

Continued

Continued from previous page

> With a little experience, you will learn to browse right to the "Consolidation" topic for this issue. This is appropriate because a purchase of greater than 50% of an entity's common stock generally results in consolidation (assuming the investee's capital structure is fairly simple). The Consolidation topic also addresses the accounting for an investor's involvement in more complex "variable interest entities."

EXAMPLE

Situation 2:

Company A (original debtor) has paid $10 million to Company B to assume its liability to pay off a 10-year loan obligation, payable to Bank. Bank agrees to release Company A from its payment obligation, but only on the condition that Company B assumes the obligation and that Company A will still pay if Company B defaults.

- Researchable question: Can Company A remove the loan obligation to Bank from its financial statements?
- Possible search terms: debt extinguishment, liability extinguishment, liability derecognition, secondary liability, guarantee, primary obligor, secondarily liable

Commentary—Situation 2:

Ultimately, the most relevant guidance for this research question would be found by keying "secondarily liable" into the search bar. Researchers would be directed to the derecognition section of the Liability Extinguishments topic (**ASC 405-20-40**), which indicates that the original debtor becomes a guarantor and must recognize a guarantee obligation.

Researchers entering "debt extinguishment" into the search bar will be led to guidance that includes links to the liability extinguishments topic; however, researchers unfortunately might overlook those links and get stuck reading a lot of guidance that does not apply.

A search of the term "guarantee" would result in guidance indicating how to value a guarantee, but such guidance doesn't indicate whether this arrangement should be recorded as a guarantee. A link to liability extinguishment guidance is available in the Relationships section of the guarantee topic.

The lesson: Often, even using the wrong search term initially will lead you to the right answer eventually. Just keep following all "leads" that appear to be potentially relevant.

Do not try to fit a round peg into a square hole; if it seems like the guidance page you are reading isn't clear in responding to your question, look for links to related content or try another search term. This is all part of the process; you will become more efficient with time.

Now
YOU
Try
1.9

Identifying Search Terms

Read the following practice scenarios, then brainstorm search terms you would use to look for relevant guidance. Identify at least two possible search terms.

1. A company ships its widgets to a customer on December 31 but has not yet collected payment from the customer. The customer has promised to pay within 30 days but has never purchased goods from the company before.

   Possible search terms to use in researching the company's accounting for the sales?

   a. _____

   b. _____

Continued

Continued from previous page

2. A customer is suing the local grocery store for a slip-and-fall incident. The grocery store believes the lawsuit will likely be considered frivolous and rejected by the court.

    Possible search terms to use in determining whether the grocery store should record or disclose the matter?

    a. _____

    b. _____

3. A landlord agrees to pay the last two months of a tenant's existing lease with another party as an inducement to have the tenant sign a lease for one of its properties.

    Possible search terms to use in determining how the tenant company should record the payment by the landlord to tenant to pay off its existing lease obligation?

    a. _____

    b. _____

Search terms can be useful not only for performing keyword searches, but also for finding a term on a page (using **ctrl+f**). Search terms can also help you maintain focus during Codification searches, as it is easy to get caught up in the guidance and lose sight of your research question. Keep your search terms at top of mind to maintain efficiency and focus during a search for guidance.

[**TIP**] from the Trenches

---

1. When is it most appropriate to use the keyword search feature?

    _____

    _____

    _____

[Now **YOU** Try 1.10]

2. If you're working with a search term that leads you to inapplicable guidance, what strategies might you use to identify other possible search terms?

    _____

    _____

    _____

Next, let's look at another search option.

Search by ASC Reference Number

Researchers can use the "Go To" feature to jump directly to specific content, by typing in the content's ASC reference number. This feature can be useful to a researcher who wants to verify a particular reference in the guidance, or for experienced researchers who have certain search paths memorized (e.g., many researchers now instinctively know that entering ASC 606-10 will take them to the revised guidance for revenue recognition)!

Figure 1-10 illustrates the use of this feature. In this example, entering **606-10-25-1** in the box at top left takes the researcher directly to revised revenue guidance.

Figure 1-10

Using the Go-To box

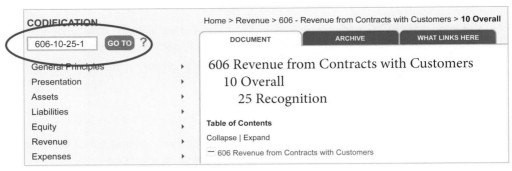

Reproduced with permission of the Financial Accounting Foundation.

Cross Reference Tab

The **Cross Reference** feature allows users to link Codification topics with the original standards that were used to populate the Codification. Users can either key in a Codification topic to find the original standard number, or they can key in the number of an original standard and be directed to the corresponding Codification topic. For example, entering ASC Topic No. 820-10 (Fair Value Measurement) into a cross-reference search directs the user to FASB Statement No. 157, *Fair Value Measurements* (**FAS 157**), as illustrated in Figure 1-11.

Figure 1-11

Using the Cross Reference feature to find the original standard corresponding to ASC 820-10

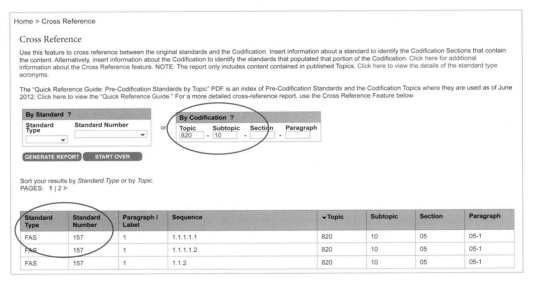

Reproduced with permission of the Financial Accounting Foundation.

The FASB continues to make its original pronouncements available on its website, as well as through a link included in the Codification (to "Pre-Codification Standards"). The abbreviations used in referring to original pronouncements are listed under the **acronyms** link within the Cross Reference page.

Master Glossary

The **Master Glossary** is another useful starting point for researchers seeking further information about a specific term. Click below any term in the Master Glossary, and you will be directed to where that term is used within the Codification. Certain terms in the Master Glossary may be duplicated or similar[8]; be sure you are consulting the definition applicable to the topic you are searching. Individual topics also include Glossaries (Section **20**), which define terms specific to that topic.

---

[8] E.g., The term *control* has different definitions depending upon which Codification topic is being referenced.

Now, let's take a moment to discuss another area that can cause confusion for beginning researchers: pending content in the Codification.

PENDING CONTENT AND EFFECTIVE DATES

What Is "Pending Content"?

When new guidance (that is, an "Accounting Standards Update") is issued by the FASB, it is added to the Codification as **pending content**.

Pending content shows up in a box, immediately following existing paragraphs in the Codification. Often, pending content has the same paragraph number as the content just above it, meaning that it will replace that guidance once it becomes fully effective. This process can take up to several years, given that companies can have different fiscal year-ends, and given that small or nonpublic entities are sometimes granted delayed effective dates. Once the pending content becomes fully effective, the previous (nonboxed) guidance will be removed from the Codification and the revised content will remain.[9]

If you see pending content directly under a paragraph that appears to be relevant to your research, click on the "Transition Guidance" link provided next to the pending content paragraph. Carefully read the transition guidance to determine whether the pending content will be effective for the transaction you are accounting for. If so, you should read the pending content in lieu of the identical paragraph number that precedes it. If pending content is in addition to existing content (for example, if there is existing content labeled par. 1-2, and pending content begins at par. 3), then consider whether this guidance should be followed in addition to existing content.

LO6 Differentiate between existing versus pending content, and understand how to interpret transition date guidance.

To illustrate the presentation of pending content in the Codification, take a look at Figure 1-12, featuring guidance from ASC 705-10 (Cost of Sales and Services). This topic was recently amended in conjunction with revised revenue recognition guidance. Using Figure 1-12, respond to the following questions.

Now [**YOU**] Try **1.11**

Figure 1-12

Pending content from ASC 705-10

25-4   For a discussion of the criteria for the recognition of revenue and the related cost of sales when the right of return exists, see the guidance beginning in paragraph **605-15-25-1**.

Pending Content: ?

Transition Date: *(P) December 16, 2017; (N) December 16, 2018* | **Transition Guidance: 606-10-65-1**

See Topic **606** on **revenue** from **contracts** with **customers**, specifically paragraph **606-10-32-10** and paragraphs **606-10-55-22 through 55-29** for the accounting for a sale with a right of return.

SUBMIT FEEDBACK ?   PERSONAL ANNOTATION ?

>   **Other Assets and Deferred Costs—Contracts with Customers**

25-4A

Pending Content: ?

Transition Date: *(P) December 16, 2017; (N) December 16, 2018* | **Transition Guidance: 606-10-65-1**

See Subtopic **340-40** for guidance on the following costs related to a **contract** with a **customer** within the scope of Topic **606** on revenue from contracts with customers:
    a. Incremental costs of obtaining a contract with a customer
    b. Costs incurred in fulfilling a contract with a customer that are not within the scope of another Topic.

Reproduced with permission of the Financial Accounting Foundation.

Continued

---

[9] FASB *Accounting Standards Codification, About the Codification* (v4.10). December 2014. Page 30.

Continued from previous page

Questions:

1. Which pending content guidance, paragraph 25-4 or 25-4A, will *replace* (aka, supersede) existing requirements? Which is *adding* new guidance? Explain.

_____

_____

2. Where in this screenshot would a researcher click to find out when the boxed content will become effective?

_____

Understanding Effective Dates

As the FASB issues new guidance, it is common for that guidance to have a delay between its issuance date and its **effective date**. This gives companies time to review and implement the new guidance. Here are three examples of how effective dates are commonly worded:

a. For fiscal years ending after December 15, 20x1

b. For fiscal years beginning after December 15, 20x1

c. For fiscal quarters beginning after December 15, 20x1

Each implies quite a different time frame. For example, assume it is the year 20x1.

- A company with a calendar year-end would have to immediately apply any new guidance with the effective date described in (*a*) above (i.e., to its 12/31/20x1 financial statements).

- On the other hand, if new guidance was issued with the effective date described in (*b*), the company would first reflect the new guidance in its 12/31/20x2 financial statements.

To check your understanding of the effective date in (*c*) above, see the **Now YOU Try** that follows.

Now YOU Try 1.12

1. Now assume that guidance has been issued with the effective date described in point *c* above. When would a company with a calendar year-end first have to reflect the new guidance in its financial statements?

_____

Let's look now at the transition guidance provided for ASC 842 (Leases), shown in Figure 1-13.

Figure 1-13

Transition guidance for recent changes to ASC 842

> **Transition Related to Accounting Standards Update No. 2016-02, *Leases (Topic 842)* and Accounting Standards Update 2018-01, *Leases (Topic 842): Land Easement Practical Expedient for Transition to Topic 842***
>
> 65-1   The following represents the transition and effective date information related to Accounting Standards Update No. 2016-02, *Leases (Topic 842)* and Accounting Standards Update No. 2018-01, *Leases (Topic 842): Land Easement Practical Expedient for Transition to Topic 842*: [**Note:** See paragraph **842-10-S65-1** for an SEC Staff Announcement on transition related to Update 2016-02.]
>
> a. A **public business entity**, a **not-for-profit entity** that has issued or is a conduit bond obligor for securities that are traded, listed, or quoted on an exchange or an over-the-counter market, and an employee benefit plan that files or furnishes financial statements with or to the U.S. Securities and Exchange Commission shall apply the pending content that links to this paragraph for financial statements issued for fiscal years beginning after December 15, 2018, and interim periods within those fiscal years. Earlier application is permitted.
>
> b. All other entities shall apply the pending content that links to this paragraph for financial statements issued for fiscal years beginning after December 15, 2019, and interim periods within fiscal years beginning after December 15, 2020. Earlier application is permitted.

Reproduced with permission of the Financial Accounting Foundation.

2. First, what *section* was this screenshot taken from (for example, Section 25—Recognition)?

_____

3. Assume your client is a public company with a calendar year-end. In what quarterly and annual periods must the company begin applying the pending content for ASC 842?

_____

PRIVATE COMPANY ACCOUNTING ALTERNATIVES IN THE CODIFICATION

Finally, recall that the Private Company Council (PCC) has been advising the FASB on areas within existing U.S. GAAP, and in the FASB's current projects, that could be simplified for private companies. The work of this council has led to an increasing number of **private company alternatives** becoming available within the Codification. Figure 1-14 illustrates scope guidance for one such alternative; this particular alternative allows private companies to *amortize goodwill*, as opposed to performing costly annual impairment tests (ASC 350-20).

> **LO7** Recognize accounting alternative guidance available for private companies.

Accounting Alternative

◉ COMBINE SUBSECTIONS ?

15-4 A private company may make an accounting policy election to apply the accounting alternative in this Subtopic. The g following transactions or activities:

    a. Goodwill that an entity recognizes in a business combination in accordance with Subtopic 805-30 after it has b

    b. Amounts recognized as goodwill in applying the equity method of accounting in accordance with Topic **323** or in recognized by entities that adopt fresh-start reporting in accordance with Topic **852** on reorganizations.

Reproduced with permission of the Financial Accounting Foundation.

Figure 1-14

Private company accounting alternative from ASC 350-20 (Goodwill)

As with other standards, unique transition guidance applies to each newly issued private company alternative. Private companies can elect to apply one, all, or none of the available alternatives.

Brainstorm: What is one potential downside of a private company electing an accounting alternative? One potential upside?

_____

_____

Now **YOU** Try **1.13**

CHAPTER SUMMARY

The FASB Codification is the essential source of authoritative accounting guidance for nongovernmental entities. SEC content is also authoritative for public companies. The Codification brings together many individual standards issued over the years in a single research database where all content has equal authority. The FASB continues to update the Codification today, through the issuance of *Accounting Standards Updates*.

Content within the Codification is organized by topic, and then further segregated into subtopics and sections. For a research effort to be thorough, certain of these sections must be included in every search. Although several methods are available for searching the Codification, users will likely find that user-directed "Browse" searches are most efficient. With practice, you will become increasingly comfortable searching the Codification.

REVIEW QUESTIONS

1. Explain what it means for the Codification's guidance to be "authoritative."
2. Explain why the Codification was developed.
3. Aside from the FASB, name three other standard-setting bodies whose guidance is included in the Codification.
4. What two organizations give the FASB the authority to establish "authoritative" accounting guidance? Explain.

5. Explain the role of industry-specific guidance in the Codification. Does it apply instead of other general Codification guidance?

6. Which search method does the FASB suggest that researchers use as a starting point when conducting research? Explain.

7. In the following template for a Codification reference, what does each group of letters represent?

XXX–YY–ZZ–PP

8. What entities does guidance in the Codification apply to?

9. Is all SEC guidance contained within the Codification, and is SEC guidance considered authoritative for all entities?

10. In which area of the Codification would a researcher begin a Browse search for the Leases topic?

11. In which area of the Codification would a researcher begin a Browse search for the Inventory topic?

12. Considering the *section* descriptions provided in the chapter, identify the section that you'd consult to determine:
    a. Whether lease guidance applies to natural resources, such as land with mineral deposits
    b. How entities should present basic EPS for continuing operations on the income statement
    c. What disclosures are required for companies preparing consolidated financial statements
    d. How to measure the effects of inventory obsolescence.

13. Which *section* might you read first if you are unfamiliar with a topic and need general information? *But*, what caution was provided regarding this section? Explain.

14. What are some possible benefits to a researcher reviewing the Implementation Guidance section (55) when conducting research?

15. Explain the numbering for S-sections from the SEC. Why does the chapter recommend that researchers consult S-99 in addition to other S-sections that might apply?

16. When including a defined term in your research paper, is it better to cite the source for this term as the Master Glossary, or the glossary located within an individual Codification topic? Explain.

17. Following is an example from ASC 350-20 (Intangibles—Goodwill), showing the organization of select paragraphs within the **Subsequent Measurement** section.

If you find guidance you are looking for under the header "Goodwill Impairment Testing and Disposal of All or a Portion of a Reporting Unit When the Reporting Unit is Less Than Wholly Owned," which other two headers should you read (at a minimum)? (For convenience, the following headers are numbered.)
    1. > Assigning Goodwill to Reporting Units
    2. > Reorganization of Reporting Structure
    3. >> Goodwill Impairment Testing by a Subsidiary
    4. >> Disposal of All or a Portion of a Reporting Unit
    5. >>> **Goodwill Impairment Testing and Disposal of all or a Portion of a Reporting Unit When the Reporting Unit is Less than Wholly Owned**
    6. >> Equity Method Investments

18. Which additional areas in the guidance are considered "required reading" for a researcher who has found general guidance in the Initial Measurement section, but who needs to be sure his or her search was thorough? (Name three other areas the researcher should consider.)

19. What is the name of the guidance currently issued by the FASB to update the Codification? Is this guidance considered "authoritative" in its own right?

20. When should a researcher rely on guidance shown under "Pending Content" instead of existing content?

21. What is the purpose of the cross-reference feature in the Codification? When might this feature be useful to a researcher?

22. What type of entity is permitted to apply accounting alternatives in the Codification? If a company elects to apply a given accounting alternative, does it mean the company must apply all of the available accounting alternatives? Explain.

EXERCISES

Use the FASB Codification to answer the following questions. There is a specific, correct answer to each of the following questions. Keep looking in the Codification until you find the reference that directly responds to these questions.

1. Suppose you wanted to understand how interest payments on a loan should be presented (classified) in the statement of cash flows.
   a. Show how you would navigate to the appropriate guidance using the "browse topics" feature on the left side of the screen. (example: liabilities-contingencies-loss contingencies-initial measurement)
   b. Now provide the numerical ASC reference for the relevant guidance, *down to the paragraph.*
   c. What search term(s) might I enter, if I wanted to perform a keyword search to locate this guidance?
   d. What is the Codification reference (ASC xxx-xxx) if I wanted specialized statement of cash flows guidance for entities in the Real Estate—Timeshare Entities' industry?

2. Describe how you would navigate to the Retirement Benefits topic, Defined Benefit Plans—Pension subtopic within the Codification.

3. In the following reference, label the Topic, Subtopic, Section, and Paragraph. Also, provide the description from the Codification for each of these (e.g., the description for Topic 842 is Leases). Here's the reference: ASC 210-20-45-1.

4. Name three of the topics listed within the Broad Transactions area.

5. a. Go to the tab entitled "cross reference" on the Codification homepage. What is the FASB Statement No. that corresponds to Topic 480-10 (Distinguishing Liabilities from Equity)?
   b. Using the "Other Sources" list on the left side of the Codification, go to pre-Codification standards. What is the full name of this FASB Statement that you identified in (a) above?
   c. Next, go to the Basis for Conclusions of the standard (as amended) that you identified in step (b). (To find this, you might start in the standard's Contents list on page 4.) Considering the introduction to the Basis for Conclusions, describe two reasons for which this standard was issued.
   d. Finally, did any FASB Board members dissent to the issuance of this FASB statement? Explain.

6. Use the "advanced search" feature (search by exact phrase) to answer part (a).
   a. Find the ASC reference (ASC xxx-xx-xx-x) for the following guidance excerpt:
      "The acquirer shall recognize separately from goodwill the identifiable intangible assets acquired in a business combination."
   b. Does this guidance (that is, in the ASC subtopic just identified) apply to private companies? Explain why or why not. Cite your sources.

For the next set of questions, identify the ASC reference—*down to the paragraph level of detail*—that you would look to for guidance on each issue.

7. Guidance on whether equity spinoff transaction guidance in the Codification applies to nonpublic entities.

8. Criteria for determining whether a lease should be classified as a finance lease or an operating lease.

9. Criteria for determining whether information about an operating segment should be reported separately (i.e., as a *reportable segment*) in the notes to a company's financial statements.

10. SEC guidance describing required disclosures in the event of a LIFO liquidation, an inventory concept.

11. Guidance stating that the issuance of stock after the balance sheet date should be treated as an nonrecognized subsequent event.

12. For number (9) above, describe the browse path you used (or would use) to locate this guidance.

For the next set of questions, answer each question using the FASB Codification and cite your source down to the paragraph[s]. Respond using complete sentences.

13. Provide two examples from the Codification of "nonauthoritative" sources of GAAP.

14. Are residual value guarantees within the scope of derivative accounting guidance?

15. a. Is SEC guidance considered authoritative GAAP? And,
    b. Is all SEC guidance housed within the Codification?

16. Should prepaid expenses be classified within current assets on the balance sheet?

17. When should an entity record the effects of changes in tax laws and rates in recording its income taxes?

18. What is the initial measurement objective when recording guarantees?

19. Within the Codification, navigate to the revised lease accounting standard.
    a. What paragraph within that topic provides transition guidance for this new topic? Also, in what period does this guidance first apply to a private company with a calendar year-end?
    b. Why does all of the content within this topic appear in boxes, as pending content? Explain.

20. Explain the need for a researcher to consider all sections of *required reading* when performing Codification research.

21. Identify search terms that you might use to research the following issues. Then, identify the browse path (down to the section) you would likely use to navigate to guidance for these issues (example of a browse path: Assets-Inventory-Overall-Initial Measurement).
    a. A popular website primarily generates revenue through ad sales. Ad buyers must pay a specified cost per click, and this cost is based on agreed-upon terms between the website and ad buyer. The typical term of an advertising arrangement is approximately one month with billing generally occurring after the delivery of the advertisement. The website must estimate the revenues it has earned but not yet collected as of the end of the period.
    b. An airline has incurred significant cost to update the interior of its aircraft, changing the configuration of seats and overhead storage space (these parts are considered part of the airframe). The airline must determine whether these costs shall be charged to expense or capitalized.
    c. A company's auditor is questioning the appropriateness of the company's healthcare cost growth rate assumption, which it uses to measure its defined benefit post-retirement medical benefits obligation.
    d. A company purchases marketable equity securities and holds the securities in a brokerage account. The company must determine how to initially measure this investment.

22. Consider the search terms you identified in the preceding question. In addition to using search terms to perform keyword searches of the Codification, what are some of the other benefits and uses for search terms? Explain.

23. Navigate to the *About the Codification* document, shown in the middle of the Codification's homepage. Using this document, describe/name:
    a. The three primary goals of the Codification.
    b. Two pronouncements of the AICPA that were considered part of the population of codified standards as of July 1, 2009 (and which are now superseded by the Codification).
    c. What content is considered *essential* versus *nonessential*. Explain.

24. Within the Cost of Sales and Services topic—Accounting for Consideration Received from a Vendor subtopic (ASC 705-20), you can find the following two headers (among others). Describe the relationship between the content that you would find within these headers.

    >   Accounting for Consideration Received from a Vendor (Supplier)

    >>   Consideration in Exchange for a Distinct Good or Service

CASE STUDY QUESTIONS

Respond fully to each question, remembering to clearly cite the guidance source for each response.

1.1 **Purchase of an Investment** An investor has just purchased a 15% share in the equity of a private company and has the right to appoint a member to the private company's 5-member board. The investor is asserting to his auditor that the investment does not qualify for the equity method of accounting since his interest is below 20%. Locate the guidance applicable to this issue and evaluate the strength of the investor's argument. Identify questions you might ask if you are the investor's auditor.

1.2 **Investments Held in Company Pension Plan** A company's existing defined benefit pension portfolio holds certain investments in private companies, which do not have a quoted exchange price. Determine what measurement basis the company must apply to these private company investments within its pension portfolio. Explain.

1.3 **Hazardous Chemical Leak** A manufacturing plant has leaked hazardous chemicals into a pond on the plant's property. The leaking of these chemicals violates state environmental protection regulations. What accounting is required for this leakage? Does the government need to be aware of the leak before the company must account for the cost of remediation?

Payable to Company Founder Jensen Inc. has a $500,000 note payable due to its founder, Jen Jensen. Ms. Jensen   **1.4**
is recently deceased and has no heirs that Jensen Inc.'s executive team is aware of. The company has asked for your
help to determine whether it is appropriate to derecognize the liability from its financial statements.

Required:

1. Respond to Jensen Inc. Describe the applicable guidance requirements, including excerpts as needed to support
   your response.
2. Next, explain how you located the relevant guidance, including the search method used and which section you
   searched within the appropriate topic.

Goodwill Accounting Alternative An "accounting alternative" is available within the Goodwill topic of the Codi-   **1.5**
fication (ASC 350-20), specifically as it relates to the subsequent measurement of goodwill. Locate this alternative,
and explain: 1) What measurement approach does the accounting alternative permit?; 2) What types of companies are
eligible to apply this accounting alternative, and where did you locate this information?; 3) How does the accounting
alternative differ from the measurement requirements for companies that do not (or cannot) elect this treatment?;
4) What was the effective date for this guidance, and where did you locate this information?

Applying Transition, Effective Date Guidance You are on the audit team for a publicly traded insurance company   **1.6**
with a calendar year-end. The company needs help understanding the FASB's recent standard (ASU 2018-12) on
insurance contracts and has asked you the following questions: 1) In what annual period are we first required to apply
the new standard? 2) In what interim period? 3) When we apply the new standard, are we required to recast comparative periods to conform to the new requirements? 4) What topic does this ASU update within the Codification? 5)
What are some of the key changes brought about by this new standard?

For each question, explain where within the guidance (ASU or Codification) you located the information.

Early Payment Discount Jones Equipment is a private company that sells and installs HVAC systems. Jones offers   **1.7**
payment terms of 2/10, n/30, where customers making payment within 10 days of installation will receive a discount
of 2% off the purchase price or must pay the full balance due within 30 days. Jones has just received payment from
a new customer who paid within the 10-day window and is thus entitled to the 2% discount. The gross sales price of
the equipment and installation, before discount, was $10,000. This discount will not result in a loss to Jones on the
sale of the product and service. Jones needs your help to determine when the 2% early-payment discount should be
recognized and how it should be recorded—for example, as a reduction in revenue or as a cost of sales?

1. Citing from the guidance as support, show the approximate journal entries that Jones would make upon installation of the equipment and upon receipt of customer payment. 2. Explain how you located the relevant guidance,
including the search method used and which section you searched within the appropriate topic.

Determining Inventory Costs Pro Packs, Inc. manufactures its own backpacks, marketed to customers primarily for   **1.8**
camping and travel needs. The company is reviewing its policy for capitalizing inventory costs and wants your help
to determine whether the following costs should be capitalized as part of the cost of inventory: 1. Canvas used in the
construction of the packs; 2. Zippers purchased from YKK (a supplier), including the cost of freight for the zippers
to be shipped; 3. Wages paid to employees operating industrial sewing machines; 4. Electric utility bills related to
operation of the plant; and 5. Contract labor paid to update and maintain the company website, through which customers can directly place backpack orders. For each cost noted, explain your position and the source you consulted.

Purchase of a Vineyard Your client has just purchased land on which it intends to build a vineyard. In doing so, the   **1.9**
client incurs the following costs: 1) land surveys; 2) costs of leveling the land; 3) installation of fencing; 4) installation of a sprinkler system. Refer to industry guidance in the Codification to determine whether these costs should
be capitalized and whether there are restrictions surrounding the capitalization period. Also, educate your client on
how the Codification classifies these different types of costs. Finally, locate one other example of a cost that may be
capitalized and explain any restrictions on the period during which the cost may be capitalized.

Falling Boxes On January 31, an improperly stacked box fell from the top shelf of a warehouse, injuring an employ-   **1.10**
ee. The employee was hit, fell, and broke his wrist. Your company self-insures for the risk of such incidents rather
than paying an insurance company to absorb the risk of such claims. The employee has been treated for his injuries
and has retained a lawyer. The lawyer has not yet filed a formal claim with the company. According to your internal
risk management team, the amount of claim likely to be sought by the employee could range between $50,000 and
$300,000. Is your company required to record a liability for this incident? When, and for what amount? What dis-
closures are required, if any?

Sale of Custom Merchandise Custom Wares is a public company that sells custom merchandise, including   **1.11**
engraved picture frames. On December 15, the company received a purchase order and payment from a customer
(Jim Burke) for the purchase of 200 custom frames. The frames will be used as a wedding favor and engraved "Jim
and Jess, 2020."

On December 30, Custom Wares shipped the completed order to Mr. Burke, and Mr. Burke received the frames via UPS on January 2. Company policy allows customers to return merchandise within 30 days for a full refund if they are not to the customer's satisfaction. Historically, Custom Wares has experienced product return rates of 2%. The frames sell for $25 each and cost the company approximately $10 each.

Custom Wares must determine whether it can recognize the revenue from the sale, when, and in what amount. For example, should Custom Wares wait until the 30-day return window lapses? Citing guidance from the Codification as support, attempt the journal entries that Custom Wares should record at the time of order, at the time of customer receipt, and—if applicable—upon expiration of the return window.

Chapter 2

The Research Process

Michael Jones has just joined the accounting policy team at Presto Hospitality (Presto), a public company in the business of operating food and beverage concessions. Presto is in the process of executing a contract related to the following proposed transaction:

> Presto has negotiated a 10-year concessions agreement with a major league baseball stadium owner (Stadium Co.). The agreement would give Presto the right and obligation to operate all of the stadium's fixed concession stands and portable food and beverage carts, to provide food and beverage service to premium seating areas (including suites), and to have hawkers selling concessions in the aisles of the stadium (Sodas! Peanuts!), collectively, the "Food and Beverage Facilities." The locations of fixed concession stands within the stadium are designated in architectural drawings included within the draft concessions agreement. The draft contract states that Stadium Co., at its option and at its cost (such as the cost to rebuild leasehold improvements), can require Presto to move its locations within the stadium.
>
> The concessions agreement will require Presto to remit 50% of its gross food sales and 52% of its gross alcohol sales to Stadium Co. in exchange for the right to operate at the stadium. Presto will also be required to make an upfront payment of $5 million to Stadium Co., which will be used toward capital improvements, build-outs, and branding of the concession facilities. Throughout the operating period of this agreement, Stadium Co. will have the right to approve all of Presto's proposed menu items, pricing, and choices of suppliers, and Stadium Co. has indicated in negotiations that it plans to actively exercise this approval authority. To be chosen as the concession provider for this stadium, Presto submitted a successful bid and was selected from a group of competing potential concessionaires.

Continued

After reading this chapter and performing the exercises herein, you will be able to

Learning Objectives

1. **List** the six steps of the research process.
2. **Identify** sources for learning about an industry, and for gathering transaction facts.
3. **Define** the research problem, through the identification of "researchable questions."
4. **Search** broadly for potentially relevant guidance.
5. **Examine** alternative viewpoints in an accounting research analysis.
6. **Justify** and document your conclusion.
7. **Identify** common decision traps and judgment biases.

Continued from previous page

Michael has been asked to evaluate the accounting implications of this draft concessions agreement. As he is new to the company, he wonders where to begin researching this issue. Should he go right to the Codification for guidance, or are there other steps he should take first?

This chapter introduces the accounting research process, an approach you can apply in practice when faced with complex research issues. Notably, our discussion of this Presto Hospitality transaction continues into the next chapter, which covers effective writing techniques.

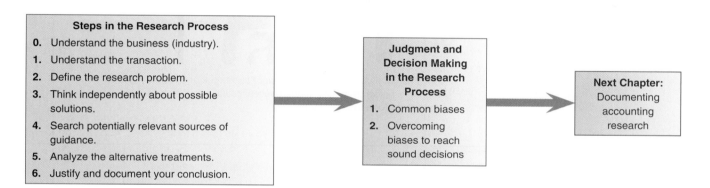

Steps in the Research Process
0. Understand the business (industry).
1. Understand the transaction.
2. Define the research problem.
3. Think independently about possible solutions.
4. Search potentially relevant sources of guidance.
5. Analyze the alternative treatments.
6. Justify and document your conclusion.

Judgment and Decision Making in the Research Process
1. Common biases
2. Overcoming biases to reach sound decisions

Next Chapter: Documenting accounting research

Organization of This Chapter

This chapter introduces the accounting research process, which is a step-by-step process that researchers can apply to a wide range of business and accounting issues. As illustrated in the preceding graphic, this process involves—first—fully understanding a transaction (within the context of a given industry), then identifying the issues, thinking through these issues, locating applicable research, considering alternatives, and—finally—reaching a thoughtful and defensible conclusion.

In applying the research process, it helps to understand some of the decision traps and biases that you may be prone to as a researcher and decision maker. Accordingly, judgment and decision-making concepts are also introduced in this chapter.

Documentation skills, also integral to accounting research, are addressed in the next chapter of this book.

When faced with research questions in practice, you'll want a plan for how to address them. You'll also want that approach to feel automatic. Take the time now to understand and practice applying the research process—this will be a tool you can call upon for years to come.

WHY USE A RESEARCH PROCESS?

As a beginning researcher, your tendency might be to dive right into authoritative guidance when faced with a research question. But your professor—and professionals—would tell you there's a better way to research. The goal of this chapter is to teach you a more thoughtful approach.

Consider the research approaches illustrated in Figures 2-1 and 2-2. Which research approach would you trust more?

Figure 2-1

Approach 1

Beginning researchers often go straight to the guidance when they receive a research question, often necessitating return trips to their supervisor for additional facts.

Figure 2-2

Approach 2

| Take time to fully understand the issue. Don't be afraid to ask questions. | Define the research question, then think through possible alternatives. | Perform research, then use this guidance to analyze alternatives. | Justify and document your conclusions. |

The research process introduced in this chapter involves broadly understanding the issues, and their context, plus thinking through the issue yourself, all *before* looking for guidance in the Codification. This chapter may sound like a lot of theory. But it's not. In practice, accounting researchers *actually* apply a similar process.

THE ACCOUNTING RESEARCH PROCESS

LO1 List the six steps of the research process.

The **accounting research process** is the step-by-step process that researchers can apply to a wide range of open-ended accounting issues encountered in practice.

The research process described in this book consists of the following steps:

Pre-Step: Understand the Business (Industry).

| 1. Understand the facts. | 2. Define the problem. | 3. Stop and think. | 4. Search for guidance. | 5. Analyze and document alternatives. | 6. Justify and document conclusion. |

Note that multiple variations of this process exist (for example, in other textbooks, in accounting firm literature, etc.); this book describes just one of many possible approaches. The approach described here is particularly geared to the beginning researcher, who may require a few extra steps in order to fully analyze an issue. Generally speaking, the similarities among the various research approaches tend to outnumber their differences.

To best understand this process, 1) first, read about it; 2) second, practice applying it to case studies. In time, the steps in this process will become second nature to you. Professionals with a mastery of this process may find themselves being asked to participate on increasingly higher-level projects—offering valuable opportunities to grow in knowledge and skills.

Pre-Step: Understand the Business (Industry)

Perform this step upon being assigned to a new client, or before starting work in a new industry.

Your first task in the research process, before you even begin understanding a specific research question, is to get to know your company's—or your client's—business. Understanding the business (or industry) gives you the appropriate context for considering company-specific accounting issues. **In other words, you first need to understand the business before you can understand the transaction.** Without preliminary research on the client's business, you risk asking questions about a transaction that are not informed.

> **LO2** Identify sources for learning about an industry, and for gathering transaction facts.

Consider this comment from a fellow accounting research instructor:

> "When I created this course I met with several Partners at Big 4 firms. One thing I heard more than once was they thought new hires lacked the ability to research and understand their client's business. Therefore, I try to teach that prior to performing accounting research we should research and understand the business itself."

The business environment, supply chain, sources of revenues and expenses, and timing of cash flows can vary greatly for different industries. Just imagine how different the accounting issues faced by an Agriculture company, versus an Airline, might be.

To address these unique accounting issues, the Codification includes an Industry area with industry-specific accounting guidance. Figure 2-3 illustrates the topics included in the Industry area, and provides examples of companies.

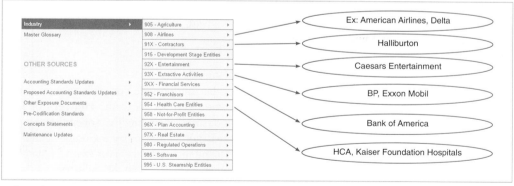

Figure 2-3

Industry-specific topics in the Codification, plus examples of companies in select industries

Reproduced with permission of the Financial Accounting Foundation.

To become more informed about an industry, your goal during this pre-step is to understand:

- What are the primary business activities of companies in this industry?
- What are key revenue sources, and costs, for companies in this industry?
- What accounting practices are unique to this industry?
- What are some of the peer group companies in this industry?

How Do I Learn About a New Industry?

AICPA Audit and Accounting Guides (**A&A Guides**) are arguably the best resource for getting to know a new industry. See Figure 2-4. These guides contain general background on the industry, including typical operations and ownership structures, guidance on auditing techniques for the industry, and accounting guidance for transactions specific to the industry.

These guides are not available for every industry, as Michael (from our opening scenario) quickly discovered. However, you can see in Figure 2-4 that this would be a valuable resource for an accountant new to the industries for which these are available.

Figure 2-4

Snapshot from the A&A Guide *Construction Contractors*

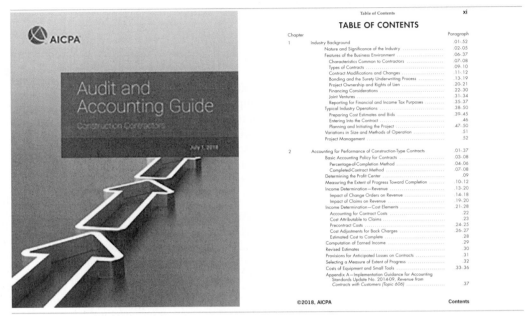

A&A Guides can be purchased directly from the AICPA, or can be accessed through certain research databases, such as the AICPA's online research system and Deloitte's *Accounting Research Tool (DART)*.

[**TIP**] **from the Trenches**

> While the *auditing* guidance in A&A Guides is authoritative, the *accounting* guidance in A&A Guides is nonauthoritative.

Suppose that you do not have access to A&A Guides. What then?

Your next best option is to consider other sources that can provide you with an overview of the industry. Your university's online library may provide you access to the **Hoovers** or **IBIS** databases, which offer a great introduction to specific industries, including their operations, supply chain, major companies, and more. If these resources are not available, try a Google search for: "Overview of Concession Industry" (or "Overview of Hospitality Industry") for example, and look for reputable industry trade organization websites designed to teach about the industry.

Additionally, you can find the names of other companies in the industry with the **Mergent Online** database, by inputting a company name then clicking on Competitors.

Finally, another excellent way to learn about an industry is to review the annual report (Form 10-K) of your client, or of another company that is a key player in the industry. To locate a company's 10-K, simply Google search "10K Halliburton", for example. Or go to the company's website, then look for their Investor Relations page.

Focus on the following sections of the 10-K to broadly learn about the company and its unique accounting issues:

▨   Business (Item 1)

▨   Critical Accounting Policies and Estimates (a component of Item 7, MD&A)

▨   Significant Accounting Policies (generally Note 1 or 2 of the financial statement footnotes)

You'll quickly realize that it would be impossible to adequately perform research without first broadly understanding the business and specific company strategy.

Recall from the opening scenario of this chapter that Michael recently joined the accounting policy team at Presto Hospitality. Imagine that Michael has come to you for advice about how to quickly get up to speed on his new industry. What resources would you recommend that he read, and specifically what sections of these resources?

> **Now**
> **YOU**
> **Try**
> **2.1**

_____

_____

_____

_____

> ### Why is *understanding the business* a pre-step?
> Don't wait until you're given your first research assignment to start understanding a company's business model and peer group. By then, the expectation will be that you're ready to go on Step 1 of the research process.
>
> The time to complete this step 0 is when you first get assigned to a client in a new industry, or during the transition period before you start as an employee of a new company. You may need to do this reading off the clock—think of it as doing your homework on the company.

Step 1: Understand the Facts/Background of the Transaction

Let's assume that your involvement in this whole transaction review process began when your supervisor dropped a contract on your desk and said: "Read this and tell me what you think the accounting should be." What would you do first?

Your first challenge in any accounting research assignment is to *fully understand* the transaction and *why* it is being entered into. Obtaining this understanding often starts with

▨   Reading transaction documents, including draft or final contracts, and

▨   Talking to parties within your organization who have knowledge of the transaction. This can help you understand the purpose of the transaction, plus provides context for any unique terms of the transaction.

After considering the two preceding resources, think about whether you understand the big picture for this transaction. Do you have a clear understanding of *who* the parties are to this transaction, and *why* they are entering into it? Do you clearly understand the *economics (financial costs and benefits)* and *cash flows* of the arrangement? Without realizing it, beginning researchers may go through several rounds of research with incomplete information, gathering additional facts each time they stop to ask ("frequent fliers" to the boss's office). Save yourself time and effort by trying to form a complete picture during this first step of the research process. It might help at this point for you to sketch out—for your own benefit—a picture of the transaction. Instructions for doing this are provided in the next chapter.

Researching the accounting for a transaction should ideally occur before the transaction takes place (and before contracts are finalized). Be careful, however. An accounting position documented based on *draft* agreements could change as contracts are edited and finalized. Changes to contracts and final drafts should be reviewed to ensure that they do not change the accounting analysis.

Once you have a working understanding of a transaction, consider whether the following resources would shed additional light on the transaction:

- Has my company undertaken any transactions similar to this in the past? If so, try to get your hands on any memos documenting the background and accounting positions taken for those transactions. This will not only save you time and effort in researching the issues, but it may also provide additional understanding of the company's business purpose in entering this transaction.

- Have peers in my industry completed similar transactions? If so, look for discussion of these transactions in
  - Peer companies' public filings (Form 10-Ks), press releases, or responses to SEC comment letters (where the company may describe to the SEC its rationale for accounting positions taken).
  - Industry-specific publications, such as whitepapers or accounting guides.

  Take note of the accounting elections or judgments addressed by your peers that may be relevant to your transaction; be aware, however, that differences in terms may exist between the transactions.

- Should specialists be involved? Certain transactions can be highly nuanced and may require the involvement of individuals with specialized knowledge. Examples of such nuanced transactions include business combinations, securitizations, so-called hybrid debt offerings, or transactions related to a company's pension obligations, to name a few. If such specialized knowledge is not available within your own company, your auditors may be a good resource. Types of specialists include
  - Technical accounting specialists
  - Actuaries
  - Valuation specialists, and
  - Legal counsel.

Any steps that you are able to take to fully understand the purpose and economics of a transaction should be taken.

In some cases, however, you might be given only limited background on an issue (verbally, or in writing) and told what to research. This may be especially true early in your career. For example, your supervisor may not want to divulge all relevant transaction facts to you, and may only be asking for your help with one aspect of the research. Even in such cases, it is helpful to go through the preceding list of steps as a sort of checklist; ask yourself: "Can I still perform this step for my limited-scope research question?" Often, even without access to contracts, many of the listed steps will still apply, such as consideration of company past practices and comparison to peer transactions.

Now
[YOU]
Try
2.2

Recall the concessions agreement described in the opening scenario of this chapter. In your opinion, what are some of the most critical resources that Michael should consider—and key questions he should ask—in his effort to understand this proposed transaction?

_____

_____

_____

_____

_____

A Final Note: Listening Skills during Step 1

Listen up! In this step of the research process, *listening skills* are key. Being assigned to this research project gives you the opportunity to reach out and learn from others in your organization (or your client's). Your supervisor, and your operations contacts, have a perspective about the company and this transaction that you do not have. This research project is your opportunity to learn from them.

In a 2017 survey of employers, listening skills were ranked as the second most important skill (out of 25) for new graduate business school hires. (Oral communication was ranked as the most important skill, with written communication ranked fourth)[i].

How can you be a better listener? It's simple: Give the person your full attention, and just listen. Be patient if the speaker communicates differently from you; focus on what is being said, not how. Don't plan your next comment or question, and don't interrupt. Take notes as necessary. Try to walk away from the conversation having learned from, and understood, what was said.

[i] 2017 Corporate Recruiters survey by the Graduate Management Admission Council.

Step 2: Define the Problem. That Is, Identify the "Researchable Question."

The next step of your research process is to define the problem; that is, identify the **researchable question(s)**. Doing so will help to focus your research efforts. Avoid long or complex questions; if your question has multiple parts, break that issue into two or more questions.

LO3 Define the research problem, through the identification of "researchable questions."

Following are examples of researchable questions that might come to mind during your initial review of a contract:

- *If my company will receive money under the contract*: Will we recognize revenue for this? Will receiving these funds cause us to incur a liability? Have we received any capital contributions? Have we entered into a lease arrangement?

- *If my company will pay money under the contract*: Have we created or purchased an asset? Have we incurred an expense? Have we entered into a lease arrangement?

- *If my company purchased an ownership interest in another entity:* Will my company have to consolidate the entity? Alternatively, should my company record an investment in the entity?

- *If the contract involves the purchase or sale of a commodity (e.g., oil, gas, gold) or currency:* Does this contract contain a derivative that requires mark-to-market accounting?

Notice that each of these question includes a topic that you could navigate to in the Codification, as a starting point for your research. For example,

- To respond to the question: "Will we recognize revenue for this?", an appropriate starting point for a browse search would be

  Revenue > Revenue from Contracts with Customers (**Topic 606**) > Overall (**10**) > Recognition (**25**)

- An appropriate starting point for the question: "Have we entered into a lease arrangement?" would be

  Broad Transactions > Leases (**Topic 842**) > Overall (**10**) > Scope (**15**)

- An appropriate starting point for the question: "Does this contract contain a derivative?" would be

  Broad Transactions > Derivatives and Hedging (**Topic 815**) > Overall (**10**) > Scope (**15**)

Look again at the questions above. Notice that, in some cases, the research question and related browse path focus on the application of general accounting methods (such as revenue recognition).

In other cases, the research questions focus on the *type of transaction* being evaluated, and therefore the browse path focuses on whether the arrangement is within the scope of transaction-specific guidance. This search focus is frequently most effective when performing research on topics listed within the Broad Transactions area of the Codification.

The questions just illustrated are provided with the intent of helping beginning researchers draw connections between contract terms and research questions. As such, these questions have been intentionally kept broad. In practice, however, it is often appropriate for questions to be more specific. For example, the question: "Will Presto account for the contract as a lease?" would likely be more effective than the broader wording: "How will Presto account for this arrangement?" As you work through the research process, you will find that you can become more specific with your questions.

Identifying the Researchable Question

Now YOU Try 2.3

Take a moment to practice identifying a single, researchable question for the following issues.

1. A company ships its widgets to a customer on December 31 but has not yet collected payment from the customer. The customer has promised to pay within 30 days but has never purchased goods from the company before.

   Researchable question? _____

2. A customer is suing the local grocery store for a slip-and-fall incident. The grocery store believes the lawsuit will likely be considered frivolous and rejected by the court. The grocery store must decide whether to record or disclose this matter.

   Researchable question? _____

3. A landlord agrees to pay the last two months of a tenant's existing lease with another party as an inducement to have the tenant sign a lease for one of its properties. The tenant needs to understand how to account for this payment.

   Researchable question? _____

Finally, additional researchable questions will often become apparent as you work through the research process. For example, assume that Michael has begun to evaluate whether Presto's arrangement involves a lease. Next, he might identify these additional questions:

- Does the concession agreement qualify for a scope exception from ASC 842 (Leases)?
- Does the concession agreement involve the right to use *identified assets*?

Once an accounting method has been selected, additional researchable questions might focus on *how to apply* the method selected. To illustrate this point, consider the following **Now YOU Try**.

Now YOU Try 2.4

Assume that Michael and his team conclude that Presto should account for this contract as a lease. Brainstorm some additional research questions that could arise as a result of this conclusion.

_____
_____
_____

Again, word your research questions as specifically as possible, as this provides a good framework for conducting research.

The remaining steps in the research process should be performed for each research question identified.

Step 3: Stop and Think: What Accounting Treatment Will Likely Be Appropriate?

The third step of the research process requires researchers to "stop and think." That is, before you turn to the Codification for guidance, stop and think on your own: What accounting treatment do *you* think would be most appropriate for this transaction or event? Coming up with your own, independent idea of how a transaction should be accounted for will help you to stay objective as you look for guidance in the Codification and can help you avoid anchoring to the first possible solution you find.

This is not your first accounting course—you have the knowledge to think through accounting issues independently. Use that knowledge now. Think through one or two accounting alternatives for this transaction that make logical sense to you, and jot down these alternatives.

Finally, it can be helpful at this point to jot down possible *search terms* (see Chapter 1) related to your researchable question and the possible accounting treatments you just identified. Doing so will help you avoid getting bogged down in Codification guidance once you start your search. Keep your research question, and your list of search terms, at top of mind in order to maintain efficiency and focus as you move to the next step of the research process.

> To illustrate the importance of this step, consider the following. I once assigned an ASC 840 lease research case (operating versus capital?) to two teams of students. The teams had to research the case, write an issues memo, then present the case to their peers.
>
> The students' peers (assigned to present different cases) were asked to read the lease case then to provide their "gut instinct" as to how they would conclude, without consulting professional literature. Believe it or not, the non-presenting students concluded more correctly on the case than those assigned to present. The presenting students anchored so quickly to the guidance that they failed to stop and think through the issues.
>
> Bottom line: Think through the accounting, and ask your gut what the answer should be, before diving into the guidance.

[TIP] from the Trenches

Step 4: Search Potentially Relevant Sources of Guidance, Copying Any Relevant Guidance into a Word Document

Now that you have given some thought to your research question, you are ready to search for applicable guidance.

LO4 Search broadly for potentially relevant guidance.

If you have a sense as to which topic might be most applicable to your research question, begin by browsing to that topic in the Codification.

To save yourself time, always start your research by locating the topic that you expect to be most relevant. If you don't know which topic is appropriate for your search, use the Codification's keyword search feature instead. Follow all leads (search results) that appear to be relevant, as the keyword may lead you to several useful sources of guidance. Know that sometimes, researching a single accounting issue can involve consideration of multiple Codification topics.

Let's return to our Presto Hospitality example, but let's back up for a moment. Assume that Michael's very first researchable question is: *Does this arrangement contain a lease?* What Codification **topic**, **subtopic**, <u>and</u> **section** would you expect to be most relevant to this issue?

Now [**YOU**] Try 2.5

Accordingly, Michael should begin his research by navigating to this guidance first.

As a beginning researcher, you may end up exploring a lot of places in the Codification before you find guidance that is directly on point. Keep track of potentially relevant guidance that you find by copying sections of the guidance into a Word document. Finding potentially relevant guidance can still be, essentially, a brainstorming exercise. Look for guidance that is either directly on point or, if not available, guidance that may be relevant by analogy (such as guidance applicable to a similar type of transaction). Be exhaustive in your search; consult all sources of *required reading,* and attempt to find all potentially relevant guidance that can be used to answer your research question. In this stage of the research process, you may also choose to consult nonauthoritative sources.

At the end of this step, review the guidance you have collected. Ideally, you will have found some that is relevant to your research question, and which you will analyze in the next step. Other sources, upon further review, may appear to be less relevant and can now be weeded out (deleted from your Word document). This locating, then weeding out, step is particularly geared toward beginning researchers. As you gain experience with research, you may find it easier to identify—as you go—whether or not a source is relevant, and whether it's worth pursuing. Eventually, you will be able to determine in real time which sources are most responsive to your research question.

Now YOU Try 2.6

Let's assume that Michael is in step 4 of the research process, searching for guidance on whether Presto's concessions agreement involves use of an *identified asset*. This is a key step in determining whether an arrangement contains a lease.

Per ASC 842-10:

> **15-3** A contract is or contains a lease if the contract conveys the right to control the use of identified property, plant, or equipment (an identified asset) for a period of time in exchange for consideration . . .

Michael also locates the following guidance on *identified assets* in the scope section:

> **>>Identified Asset**
>
> **15-9** An asset typically is identified by being explicitly specified in a contract. However, an asset also can be identified by being implicitly specified at the time that the asset is made available for use by the customer.

> **>>>Portions of Asset**
>
> **15-16** A capacity portion of an asset is an identified asset if it is physically distinct (for example, a floor of a building or a segment of a pipeline that connects a single customer to the larger pipeline). A capacity or other portion of an asset that is not physically distinct (for example, a capacity portion of a fiber optic cable) is not an identified asset, unless it represents substantially all of the capacity of the asset . . .

Walk Michael through the rest of step 4. What other guidance (authoritative or nonauthoritative) and what other sections in ASC 842 (e.g., Recognition, Measurement, or other sources of *required reading*) should he scan for additional guidance on this issue?

_____

_____

_____

_____

A Final Note: Avoiding Distractions during Step 4

Caution: This step 4 is the part of the research process where you may be most at risk for distractions.

Reading authoritative literature, such as the Codification, is mentally strenuous. You're going to need a quiet setting, free of distractions.

Continued

Continued from previous page

> *Consider this: A study by UC-Irvine professor Gloria Mark showed that each time an office worker was interrupted on a task (such as by responding to an email), it took on average 25 minutes to return to that task. Researchers in other studies have found that 40% of the time, delayed tasks are not resumed right after the interruption.*[1, 2]
>
> In other words, not only will interruptions slow you down, but they may derail you from the research project altogether. Wouldn't you rather just get this research done now?
>
> Your best bet: Find a quiet place to sit (the upper floors of the library are great). Turn your phone on airplane mode to avoid beeps and alerts, and close your email browser. Set aside at least a full hour; you'll need at least this amount of time to conduct really thoughtful research.
>
> If you do stop research to respond to an email, 1) keep your research windows open, and 2) jot down on a Post-it where you left off: *Next: Search ASC 842 for "identified asset."* Stick the Post-it right in front of your keyboard. These two small actions will improve your chances of resuming research after an interruption, and will minimize your mental recovery time.
>
> (In the field of "interruption science"—yes, it's a thing!—this is described as helping to jog your prospective memory. Before dealing with an interruption, remind yourself of the step you plan to tackle next.)

Step 5: Analyze Alternatives, Documenting Your Consideration of Each

Now that you have found guidance that appears to be relevant, the next step is to **analyze** that guidance, or to evaluate how the guidance applies to your research question. This process can involve judgment; that is, guidance in the Codification may not offer specific answers to your precise issue, or the Codification may allow for alternative accounting treatments. In such circumstances, it is essential for a researcher to clearly identify and analyze the relative merits of the alternatives available.

LO5 Examine alternative viewpoints in an accounting research analysis.

Sometimes, "weighing alternatives" can also mean thinking critically about whether a certain treatment is, or is not, met. In other words, don't just assume that an accounting treatment you find in the Codification is applicable. You must fully investigate the guidance before concluding that its use is acceptable. Consider the phrase **"You don't know what you don't know."**

For example, if a defined term is included within a paragraph you're evaluating, carefully review whether your arrangement meets the definition provided for that term. Or, go back to re-check the scope of the guidance you're reading. Be open to the possibility that the treatment you're considering might not apply.

To illustrate this point, complete the following **Now YOU Try** exercise, considering the facts presented in the opening scenario of this chapter.

Recall in the previous step (Step 4) that Michael was searching for guidance on whether Presto's concession agreement involved an *identified asset.* Based on additional research, Michael determined that an identified asset is present if 1) Presto will have the right to use a *physically distinct* portion of an asset and 2) the supplier does not have a substantive right of substitution (see par. 15-10).

Now
YOU
Try
2.7

>>> Substantive Substitution Rights

15-10 Even if an asset is specified, a customer does not have the right to use an identified asset if the supplier has the substantive right to substitute the asset throughout the

Continued

---

[1] Mark, G., Gonzalez, V. M., and Harris, J. *No task left behind? Examining the nature of fragmented work.* In CHI '05: Proceedings of the SIGCHI Conference on Human Factors in Computing Systems, pages 321–330, (New York: ACM Press, 2005).

[2] O'Connail, B. and Frohlich, D. *Timespace in the workplace: Dealing with interruptions.* CHI '95 Conference on Human Factors in Computing Systems, Extended Abstracts, pages 262–263 (New York: ACM Press, 1995).

Continued from previous page

> period of use. A supplier's right to substitute an asset is substantive only if **both** of the following conditions exist:
>
>   a. The supplier has the practical ability to substitute alternative assets throughout the period of use (for example, the customer cannot prevent the supplier from substituting an asset, and alternative assets are readily available to the supplier or could be sourced by the supplier within a reasonable period of time).
>   b. The supplier would benefit economically from the exercise of its right to substitute the asset (that is, the economic benefits associated with substituting the asset are expected to exceed the costs associated with substituting the asset). [Emphasis added]

Referring to the guidance in par. 15-9, 15-16, and 15-10, analyze the following judgmental issues.

1. Is the portion of an asset that Presto has the right to use physically distinct? Explain.

_____

_____

_____

2. Does the stadium owner (supplier) have a substantive substitution right? Explain.

_____

_____

_____

As we'll discuss further in the next chapter, any reasonable alternative or indicator that you weigh (positively or negatively) in evaluating an issue should be documented. In this case, Michael's documentation should highlight both the reasons for and against his conclusion.

In some cases, two acceptable alternatives may appear to be available, and it may not be clear from the authoritative guidance which should be used. In such cases, you must weigh the relative merits of each alternative, considering the following:

- If authoritative guidance (i.e., the Codification) does not express a preference as to which alternative should be used, do nonauthoritative sources (e.g., accounting firm publications) address this issue?
- Does one alternative appear to better reflect the economics of the transaction (to users of the financial statements)?
- Which alternative is most consistent with the company's prior practices, if the company has entered into similar transactions in the past?
- Is this position consistent with the positions elected by peers in my company's industry?
- Have I vetted this accounting position with the appropriate levels of management?
- Finally, do our auditors agree with this treatment?

Document all factors considered in your analysis of the alternative treatments. Start with the guidance you collected from your search of the Codification, providing discussion (in your own words) of how you considered that guidance relative to your company's fact pattern. After you have presented the authoritative guidance, next you should document all "other" factors considered in your analysis (including any meaningful consideration you gave to the bulleted items just listed).

Finally, be wary of selecting an alternative that represents a departure from a past practice of your company, or of companies in your peer group. Such a departure should be addressed in your analysis, as well as discussed with management and your auditors. Your company may risk being questioned by investors or by the SEC if you elect a position (on a material transaction) that is inconsistent with past practices or unique among those in your industry.

The next chapter describes how the researcher should document key factors considered—both from authoritative and nonauthoritative sources—in his or her written analysis of an accounting issue.

Step 6: Justify and Document Your Conclusion

The final step of the research process is to reach a conclusion—that is, determine which accounting treatment is most appropriate given the authoritative guidance and, if applicable, other key factors you have analyzed. Next, clearly document this conclusion, summarizing salient points from your analysis as justification for your position.

> **LO6** Justify and document your conclusion.

The next chapter provides guidelines for documenting conclusions.

In addition to fully analyzing the literature and considering alternatives, the SEC's staff have suggested that preparers should support accounting judgments by considering *how the selected treatment reflects the economic substance and business purpose* of the transaction.[3] At this point of the research process, pause to reflect upon whether your accounting conclusion appropriately reflects the substance of the transaction.

However if, when you reach this step, you have inadequate information to reach a conclusion, consider whether you obtained sufficient information in the previous steps. Once a robust analysis has been performed, and sufficient sources have been considered, you should be able to point to key factors from the analysis as support for the conclusion reached.

Refer back to your analysis in the preceding **Now YOU Try**.

> **Now**
> **YOU**
> **Try**
> **2.8**

1. What is your preliminary conclusion regarding whether the concessions agreement conveys the right to use an *identified asset*?

   _____

   _____

   _____

2. Alternatively, are there additional questions you need to ask before you feel comfortable concluding on this research question?

   _____

   _____

   _____

Finally, note that Michael will need to monitor any changes that are made to this draft contract, then should carefully review the final, executed agreement to ensure that it is consistent with his previous research.

You now understand how to apply the research process. But one more thing. Every step of this process—every decision you make—could be subject to your own behind-the-scenes decision prejudices. Let's take a look now at a topic that is catching the interest of industries from law, to medicine, to investing, to our own profession.

JUDGMENT AND DECISION MAKING—A BRIEF INTRODUCTION

You may not even be aware of it, but in each step of the research process, your judgments may be prone to silent prejudices, or **biases**.[4]

> **LO7** Identify common decision traps and judgment biases.

These biases are part of our human nature. Each day, we are faced with large volumes of information, and it's normal for our minds to apply mental shortcuts in order

---

[3] Final Report of the Advisory Committee on Improvements to Financial Reporting to the United States Securities and Exchange Commission, page 95. August 1, 2008.

[4] Select resources that were consulted in developing this discussion are listed at the end of this chapter, under Additional References.

to filter and process this information. These shortcuts can greatly influence how we make decisions. Yes—we are talking about how *psychology* actually influences the judgments we make as accountants!

Today, accounting firms and professional organizations alike are realizing that—in order to make sound professional judgments—it's critical that we apply a consistent research process, *and* we must be aware of common decision traps. This focus is not surprising. A 2008 report from the SEC indicated that our profession needs more guidance in the area of professional judgment, in light of increases in principles-based accounting guidance, subjectivity in measurements, and regulatory oversight of the profession.[5]

It won't be enough, if a regulator asks your company about a material, highly judgmental position, for you to argue that you applied the guidance that seemed the most on point. Rather, you'll have to be able to demonstrate the *quality* of your judgment—that your *process* for evaluating the issue was robust, and that you considered an appropriate mix of factors in reaching your ultimate conclusion. To do this, it helps to be aware of some common biases that can impact your professional judgment.

Common Biases

- **Confirmation bias**: Our inclination to seek (or weight more heavily) information supporting our existing viewpoint, and to downplay (or minimize) information supporting different options.
  - Example: After the client offers up his initial thoughts on an accounting judgment, his auditor inadvertently looks for more guidance that confirms the client view, as opposed to guidance that could oppose the client's position.
  - Investors who have a positive feeling about a company tend to focus on information about the company that confirms their prior beliefs.

- **Availability bias:** The tendency to weight more heavily that information which is readily available (or mentally accessible), and to overlook information which takes more time or effort to gather. Examples:
  - You generally feel as though the U.S. economy is improving, based in part on the fact that you recently received a raise.
  - Asked to come up with reasons for budget variances, managers tend to think of examples from recent experiences they've had.

Also related is **recency bias**, or tending to give more weight to information that you received most recently.

- **Anchoring and Adjustment:** The tendency to fixate on initial information received, and failing to adjust adequately for subsequent information. Such as fixating on a number we observe early on, then later comparing this to every other number we consider.
  - Example: If I asked you whether you thought today's temperature would be hotter or colder than 65 degrees, your responses might be closer to this number than if I had not provided this initial anchor point.
  - Asked in 1983 (when the prime interest rate was 11%) if the prime interest rate in 6 months would be above or below 8%, respondents in a study provided responses closer to this anchor point (10.5%) than respondents who were given an initial estimate of 14% (they guessed 11.2%), or given no initial estimate (they guessed 10.9%).[6]

- **Group think:** Prioritizing the views of the most vocal, most respected, or most senior, member of a group. Or agreeing too readily to a path in the interest of group harmony, without independently thinking through an issue or challenging the group's initial path.
  - Example: An accounting professor assigned a group of students to perform a gross vs. net revenue analysis using ASC 605. The group came back having analyzed just one

---

[5] Final Report of the Advisory Committee on Improvements to Financial Reporting to the United States Securities and Exchange Commission, August 1, 2008.

[6] Edward Russo, J. and Paul Schoemaker, J.H. *Winning Decisions*, page 95 (Currency Doubleday, 2002).

weak reporting indicator (credit risk) out of 11 possible indicators that could have been evaluated. How could this have happened, if all individuals were independently thinking through this case, or challenging each other's views? (The group, by the way, reportedly got along very well.)

■ **Hindsight bias:** Thinking—after the fact, once the outcome is known—that you would have made the right decision, or that you knew the right answer all along. Or viewing an event as more foreseeable after the fact than prior to the event.

● Example: An auditor who exhibits professional skepticism when evaluating an inconsistency may tend to be rewarded (by the client and his own manager) if a misstatement is found, but penalized for exhibiting skeptical behavior if no misstatement is found.[7]

■ **Escalation of commitment:** Staying with a decision even when you suspect or have evidence that the decision is wrong. That is, not "cutting your losses" once it's clear a decision is not working.

● Example: Internal auditors involved in an initial decision related to budgeting were more inclined to stay the course, making final decisions consistent with their initial decisions but which differed from internal auditors who made only a final decision on the same budget issue.[8]

● An investor buys a stock expecting its price to rise. Instead, the price falls and the investor ends up pouring more money into the failing stock than initially planned, in an attempt to justify and recoup the initial investment losses.

Notably, these are just a few of the many possible biases that can influence your decision making. Just imagine how these biases could impact each step of the research process, from deciding which facts to gather, to identifying alternatives, to reaching a conclusion.

Identifying Biases in Your Own Decision Making

Think of a recent decision you've made, either in a personal or professional context. What is one bias that may have affected your decision-making approach? Describe.

_____

_____

_____

Describe one step of the research process that could be impacted by decision biases. Explain.

_____

_____

_____

Now
YOU
Try
2.9

How Do You Overcome These Biases? (To Reach a Sound Decision?)

To overcome judgment biases, first be aware that such biases exist. Next, obtain information and viewpoints from a variety of sources. Seek information that will challenge your existing views, or which offers a different perspective. Listen and understand when someone disagrees with you. And finally, applying a systematic research process will help you evaluate issues carefully and methodically. Your best evidence of this systematic process is high-quality documentation, as we'll discuss in the next chapter.

Challenge your existing views by asking *disconfirming questions*, or questions that explore opposing views. Consider this example, from the book *Winning Decisions*:

---

[7] Brazel, Jackson, Schaefer, and Stewart. Hindsight Bias and Professional Skepticism: Does the End Justify the Means?, (Abstract). A working paper. November 2013. Retrieved from http://www3.nd.edu/~carecob/Workshops/13-14Workshops/Brazel%20Paper.pdf

[8] Brody, R. and Kaplan, S. "Escalation of Commitment Among Internal Auditors," *Auditing: A Journal of Practice & Theory*, 1996, pages 1–15.

> If [an investment analyst] thinks the disposable diaper business is becoming less price competitive, for example, he will ask executives a question that implies the opposite, such as "Is it true that price competition is getting tougher in disposable diapers?" This kind of question makes him more likely than competing analysts to get the real story.[9]

When it comes time to reach a decision, focus on the issues that are most material. What matters most in this decision, and therefore what information is most important to consider? In many cases, reaching a decision will require the team to discuss and debate reasonable alternatives. Some decision researchers favor systematic techniques, such as importance-weighted **decision matrices**, where numerical values are assigned to the importance of each decision criterion. Increasingly, accounting firms are issuing decision frameworks which outline their firm policies for applying proper professional judgment (such as the KPMG *Professional Judgment Framework*).

In short, make sure that you gather sufficient, diverse information to make a high-quality decision. Then, have an attitude of professional skepticism toward even your own judgments.

Learn from Your Mistakes (and Successes!)

Finally, much of our ability to make quality professional judgments comes from experience. Let's face it—you won't get every issue right the first time, especially early on in your career. Becoming a great accounting researcher involves a steep learning curve. To fast-track your learning, take the time to reflect—after the fact—on your mistakes and successes.

For example, if you recommend an accounting position that is later rejected or disproven, perform a *root cause analysis* of sorts, and review your process for coming to this conclusion. Was it flawed in some way? Did you fail to consider enough alternatives, or did you anchor too quickly to a solution?

You can also learn from projects that were successful. What process steps did you take that resulted in a favorable outcome? What lessons can you apply to future projects?

Writing your learnings down can be so simple—I'm a fan of Post-it notes. Simply jot down the key lesson learned and stick it on the wall ("Remember to check Section 55 Implementation Guidance"), until you feel like you've committed the lesson to memory. You might consider maintaining a brief Word document log of successes, as this list can be valuable at performance evaluation time.

Now YOU Try 2.10

Brainstorm, then briefly describe, a "lesson learned" that you've experienced already, in your brief career-to-date as an accounting researcher.

_____

_____

CHAPTER SUMMARY

This chapter introduced you to a step-by-step approach that you can apply to a range of research challenges. Your mission now is to practice using this approach, so that you'll be ready to shine when you have the opportunity to perform research professionally.

As you apply the research process described in this chapter, keep in the back of your mind some of the common judgment biases we discussed, as these can impact the choices you make in applying the research process. As discussed, your best defense against judgment biases is, first, awareness that these biases exist and next, application of a consistent, high-quality research process. As you gain experience as a researcher, take the time to identify lessons learned.

---

[9] Russo and Schoemaker, page 87.

REVIEW QUESTIONS

1. What is the accounting research process? What steps are involved in this process?
2. Why use a research process?
3. Why is it important to know a company's business before performing research on a given transaction?
4. What information should you try to understand, during the pre-step of understanding the business?
5. Name three of the resources recommended for getting to know a company's business or industry.
6. In what sections of a 10-K should a researcher look for background on a company's business and industry accounting issues?
7. What's the ideal timing for completing "step 0" of the research process?
8. Identify three resources a researcher might consult when gathering facts and background necessary to understand a transaction.
9. Why are listening skills highlighted as important for success during step 1 of the research process?
10. Why is it important to identify the "researchable question(s)" early in the research process?
11. Explain some of the ways that a researcher may revise or refine his or her research questions as he or she works through the research process.
12. What is a benefit of performing step 3 of the research process: *stop and think*?
13. Describe the process recommended in step 4 (search for guidance), for collecting then narrowing down guidance.
14. Complete the following sentence from the chapter's description of step 4. "Know that, sometimes, researching a single accounting issue can involve consideration of _____."
15. What strategies does the chapter offer for avoiding distractions when performing research?
16. Name four resources (or questions) a researcher might consider when weighing alternative accounting treatments.
17. What is one example of a judgment encountered by Michael in his consideration of whether Presto's contract involves an *identified asset*?
18. Explain the final step of the research process. Should additional evidence be gathered at this stage?
19. What caution does the chapter offer about accounting conclusions reached based on draft contracts?
20. What is a bias, and how might biases affect how you apply the research process?
21. Name the six biases described in this chapter, and briefly describe each.
22. Name three strategies for overcoming biases.

EXERCISES

1. You have just been assigned to provide client services to the following entities. For each, identify three resources you could consult in order to better understand the company's business model and industry.
    a. Pfizer
    b. Southwest Airlines
    c. Caesars Entertainment

2. For the first company in the preceding question, Pfizer, use a library database to:
    a. Identify two competitors (aka, major companies in the industry).
    b. Next, look for an industry description page. Quoting verbatim from the database, name one interesting fact about this industry.

3. Look up the AICPA Audit & Accounting Guide *Airlines*, then review the full table of contents in the Preface of this guide. Imagine that you've just been assigned to the audit of an airline. Name two topics from this guide that you might read (or skim) in advance of the engagement, and explain why you chose these.

4. Understanding the facts/background of a transaction: Caesars Entertainment is in negotiations to purchase a new hotel. You are an analyst in the accounting policy department and are in the first step of the research process (understanding the facts/background of the transaction). Identify three resources you could consult to gather additional background/precedent for this issue.

5. You are once again in the first step of the research process (understanding the facts). Now, your company is look-ing to repurchase some of its outstanding stock at a fixed price on a certain future date. You are about to attend a meeting between representatives of your company's Treasury department and a bank. Identify three resources you could consult, or questions you might ask of others on your team or in the organization, to gather additional background/precedent for this issue before you attend the meeting.

Identify at least one researchable question for each of the following issues (in questions 6–12).

6. A cable network has just entered into an agreement granting it the right to show reruns of a hit TV series. In exchange for this right, the network must pay the TV show's creators a fee each time the show airs.

7. An online restaurant booking site sells a $100 meal voucher, good for $100 toward a meal at Randall's Steak-house, to a customer for $60. When the customer presents the voucher to Randall's Steakhouse, the restaurant booking site must remit $50 to Randall's, retaining $10.

8. A company's auditor is questioning the appropriateness of the company's discount rate assumption, which it uses to measure its defined benefit pension obligation.

9. Coal, Inc. has paid $10 million to a waste disposal company to clean a site originally contaminated by Coal, Inc. through its operations and to assume its environmental liability (currently recorded as an $10 million liability on Coal's financial statements). State regulators have signed off on the liability transfer and now look to the waste disposal company as the responsible party for the cleanup.

10. Automotive, Inc. has announced the sale of its Truck Division's three plants, along with planned layoffs of the Truck Division's employees. Automotive, Inc. is hoping to segregate the results of the Truck Division's opera-tions in its financial statements. Identify at least two possible research questions.

11. Your company is planning to issue equity securities with attached call options, where the company can repur-chase the securities at a specified price if future events occur.

12. For the following researchable question, identify two additional questions that might arise as the researcher digs deeper into the research topic. Assume that a company has just sold a portfolio of mortgage loans in exchange for cash and certain retained interests in the loans receivable. The initial question: Can the company record the transfer as a sale?

13. Stop and think. In this example, you'll be asked to stop and think about an issue, then to search the Codification for applicable guidance.
    a. Stop and think. Your company sells seasons passes to a waterpark that it owns. The passes are good from June 1 to September 30 of a given year. The company must determine the appropriate pattern of recognition for recording this revenue. What does your instinct tell you?
    b. Now, perform research within the Codification to find guidance on this issue. How does the authoritative guidance describe this issue?
    c. Finally, consider: Was your instinct consistent with the guidance for this issue? How did this instinct help you evaluate the guidance you found?

14. Identifying alternative accounting treatments: A joint venture was just formed, and one of the venturers (com-panies that invested in the JV) contributed a technology patent with a basis of $5 million and an estimated fair value of $9 million. List two accounting measurement alternatives available for the joint venture to recognize the contributed patent. Explain. (Notably, the Codification does not directly provide guidance for this issue, so your goal during this exercise is just to brainstorm.)

15. What are two types of "Accounting Changes" described in the Codification? Identify these "alternative" types of accounting changes, and cite where you found these listed in the Codification.

For each of the following sample scenarios (in questions 16–19), identify one or more biases that could be at play, then explain.

16. A judge ruling in a securities fraud case found a corporation guilty of misleading investors because the com-pany's disclosures predicted that a new drug would likely receive FDA approval years before the actual approval came through. What bias may have been at play for the judge in reaching this ruling?

17. Growth rates in sales had slowed versus the prior year. A task force was convened that consisted of senior vice presidents from across the company, plus one executive vice president (the COO). The COO came to the meet-ing prepared to offer a solution. When she did, the group agreed it was the appropriate path forward and set in motion a plan to implement her recommendation.

18. Upon adoption of the new revenue standard, a company wrestled with a gross versus net accounting policy judg-ment and ultimately rationalized that it should likely continue its current position unless there was a compelling reason in the guidance to change.

19. Smith Corp. is testing one of its manufacturing plants for impairment following a decline in real estate values for the market in which the plant is located. Smith Corp. has submitted its estimate of undiscounted future cash flows to its auditors to ask whether the company's view of the value appears reasonable.

20. The six decision traps and biases are not an all-inclusive list. Perform an Internet search for one other bias that you believe could be applicable to accounting or auditing, and which was not named in this chapter. In two or three sentences, explain this bias and its potential application to our profession.

CASE STUDY QUESTIONS

Researching Presto's Industry Recall Presto Hospitality, the (fictitious) concessions company introduced in this chapter. Assume that you have just been assigned to work on the Presto audit team, but you do not have prior experience in this industry. You need to do a little homework before the engagement begins.   2.1

1. Using an online library database that is available to you (such as Hoovers or IBIS), research and respond to the following:
   - What industry or industries would you describe as most closely related to Presto's business?
   - What are some key companies (competitors) in this industry?
   - What are key sources of revenue for companies in this industry?
   - What can you learn about this industry's supply chain?
   - What information can you find on industry growth trends and forecasts?
   - What is one other industry-specific fact you learned (e.g., industry jargon, analyst call preparation questions, etc.)?

2. Next, brainstorm: What is one other source you might consult for background on this industry prior to beginning the audit?

Presto Hospitality—Research Questions   2.2

1. *a.* List the research questions that Presto would need to evaluate to determine whether its concession agreement is a lease.
   b. Next, list the research questions that would result if Presto were to determine the arrangement is a lease.
   c. Finally, list the research questions that would result if Presto were to determine the arrangement is *not* a lease.

2. Stop and think: What accounting treatment do you think is likely to be most appropriate?

3. What are some of the implications of the different alternatives that you identified (such as in your list of research questions)?

Presto Hospitality—Scoping Assume that Presto concludes the arrangement is not a lease. Next, in selecting an appropriate framework for evaluating the Presto Hospitality concessions agreement, evaluate whether this arrangement should be considered a *Collaborative Arrangement*. What are the implications of an arrangement falling within the scope of this guidance? In addition to researching the guidance, stop and think: Does this guidance intuitively make sense for this situation?   2.3

Presto Hospitality—Identified Asset Question Recall from the case facts in the Presto Hospitality example that the concessions agreement includes architectural drawings noting the location of fixed concession stands within the stadium. Research whether the fixed concession stands would still be considered *identified assets* if the contract did not include these drawings. For example, assume the contract states: "Concession Provider has the right to operate concession stands and portable carts within the Stadium (the "Food and Beverage Facilities") as well as the right to have hawkers selling food and beverage and the right to serve food and beverages in suites and club seating areas." Use excerpts from the Codification to evaluate and conclude upon whether the concession stand locations would still be considered *identified assets*.   2.4

As necessary, identify additional questions you might ask—or facts you might gather—in order to fully research this question.

Presto Hospitality—Lease Scope Research Research this question: Is Presto entitled to *substantially all economic benefits from use of the identified assets*? What is the significance of this question (in other words, what happens if the answer to this question is yes? What if the answer is no?). You may need to review the sample memo at the end of Chapter 3 for additional guidance on Presto's identified assets. In researching this question, in addition to the facts presented previously, consider also that Stadium Co. can require Presto to source supplies from sponsors of the stadium (Stadium Co.'s "official sponsors").   2.5

As necessary, identify additional questions you might ask—or facts you might gather—in order to fully research this question.

2.6   Presto Hospitality—Upfront Payment The Presto Hospitality case facts note that Presto is required to make a $5 million upfront payment to Stadium Co., and these funds will be used toward capital improvements, build-outs, and branding of the concession facilities. Research: What is the accounting for the $5 million upfront payment? How does this accounting change if this is a lease versus if the arrangement is determined to not be a lease? Do companies in this industry describe similar payments in their 10-K disclosures?

2.7   Industry Research, Lease Adoption In their adoption of ASC 842 (Leases), companies in the travel and hospitality industry debated the question of whether *hotel rooms are leases*.

Apply the research process to this question as follows:
    a. Research the industry—what are some companies that own or operate hotels?
    b. Locate disclosures from one of these companies to get a better understanding for how they describe hotel room rentals (both from a business and an accounting perspective). Review, for example, the latest 10-K for one of the companies you identified.
    c. Define the research question.
    d. Stop and think: What answer makes sense to you, and what are the potential implications of this judgment?
    e. Search for guidance. What guidance does the Codification offer that might address this issue?
    f. Analyze and document the alternatives.
    g. Conclude and justify your position.

2.8   Identifying Researchable Questions *Facts:* Imports Inc. is a U.S. public company and has a calendar year-end. Imports purchases auto parts from Korea and sells them to domestic car dealerships around the U.S. On November 1, 20X1, Imports received a shipment on account of $400,000 worth of shocks and struts from its Korean supplier. Unfortunately, the parts were defective. Faced with commitments to deliver working parts to its own customers, Imports paid $200,000 on 11/15/X1 to a domestic third party to fix the defective parts. However, even after the repair effort, the shocks and struts remained defective.

Imports has not yet paid the Korean company for the parts purchased.

In early December, Imports requested repayment from the manufacturer for its costs of repair ($200,000). However, when the manufacturer refused to pay, Imports sued the manufacturer on 12/15/X1 for its amount invested ($200,000) plus an additional $100,000 for lost revenues.

On February 2, 20X2, a U.S. court ruled in favor of Imports, awarding Imports Inc. $300,000, payable ratably in three monthly installments to begin on 2/15/X2.

Required:
1. Identify Import Inc.'s researchable questions as of 12/31/X1 related to this series of issues.
2. Identify Import Inc.'s researchable questions as of 2/2/X2 related to this series of issues.

2.9   Change in Estimate versus Error Correction *Facts:* Your company, PlumbAll, provides routine and quick-response plumbing services to a range of corporate customers. Customers are expected to pay on the first of each month, in advance of receiving services. One of your customers is a private school that has been a longtime customer. The customer has not paid for the last four months of services (September–December 20X1); nevertheless, to maintain a positive relationship, your company continued to provide services during that time. Your company ceased providing services in January 20X2 and found out in that same month that the school filed for bankruptcy in August. You now believe that collection of the missed payments is extremely unlikely.

Your company has already issued financial statements to lenders (for the period ending 12/31/X1) that reflected revenue and a corresponding account receivable related to this customer of $11,000 per month for services provided to this customer. Those financial statements also reflected the company's standard allowance (reserve) amount on receivables of 3% of sales. In total, your company's average monthly sales amount to $300,000.

Required:
1. Evaluate whether receipt of this information indicates you have a *change in estimate* or whether the customer's bankruptcy results in this event being considered *an error in previously issued financial statements*.
2. Describe the accounting treatment required by the Codification for each alternative. Support your explanations with draft journal entries.
3. Briefly state which treatment appears to be more appropriate given the circumstances, describing any assumptions you made in concluding.

2.10   Hone Your Listening Skills The chapter mentioned that an important part of the research process is learning to *listen* to others, so that you can learn from them. Conduct a two-minute interview with a peer or friend who is studying a different field. Ask that person to teach you something that they find interesting about their field. For two minutes, work very hard to listen attentively. Document the conversation, describing what you learned. Finally, describe a circumstance in which you think these listening skills could benefit you as an accounting professional.

You Create the Case (Applying the Accounting Research Process) On your own, create a fictitious fact pattern (accounting problem/business issue) to which you can apply the accounting research process. If you can, use a fact pattern based on a real situation that you've encountered professionally. Alternatively, the following sources may help you generate ideas: (1) The Codification: browse for guidance, then "back into" a fact pattern; (2) recent business news articles (e.g., from the *Wall Street Journal*); (3) discussions with small-business owners; or (4) corporate annual reports.

2.11

Required:

1. Describe the fact pattern.
2. Identify at least 1 researchable question for this fact pattern.
3. Brainstorm the likely answer to the question.
4. Locate the applicable Codification reference. Describe the requirements, plus any alternatives available.
5. Briefly describe your conclusion.

ADDITIONAL REFERENCES

1. Kahneman, Daniel. *Thinking, Fast and Slow*. Farrar, Straus and Giroux, 2013.
2. Russo, J. Edward and Schoemaker, Paul J.H. *Winning Decisions: Getting It Right the First Time.* Crown Business, 2001.
3. Fay, Rebecca. "I'm not biased, am I?" *Journal of Accountancy*, February 1, 2015.
4. *Elevating Professional Judgment in Auditing and Accounting: The KPMG Professional Judgment Framework.* 2011, KPMG.

Chapter 3

Creating Effective Documentation

Recall Michael, the accounting policy analyst at Presto Hospitality who was introduced in the previous chapter. Now that Michael has learned a step-by-step research process to apply to Presto's draft concessions agreement, his next challenge is to prepare thoughtful documentation of the accounting issues identified.

Michael's supervisor has asked him to prepare an issues memo that documents the accounting for this transaction. His documentation should walk through the path he took to concluding on whether Presto's concessions agreement contains a lease and—if not—what accounting is most appropriate for the arrangement.

In practice, *documenting* accounting research is integral to the process of *performing* research. So Michael would have prepared much of this documentation while performing his research. However, this chapter specifically focuses on writing. This chapter covers writing conventions, style, and tips that are particular to technical accounting research. Read on, and find out what tips we can offer Michael on preparing a memo that professionally addresses his company's proposed transaction.

Learning Objectives

After reading this chapter and performing the exercises herein, you'll be able to do the following:

1. **Explain** the importance of documentation.

2. **Draft** effective emails to communicate the results of limited-scope research.

3. **Formulate** an effective Facts section and Issues list in an accounting research memo.

4. **Prepare** an effective research analysis, including consideration of alternative viewpoints, and a well-supported conclusion.

5. Properly **reference** passages from the Codification.

6. **Communicate** using professional style.

Organization of This Chapter

This chapter begins by discussing the key role that documentation plays in the performance—and preservation—of accounting research. Next, the chapter describes how to (1) draft effective emails and (2) prepare technical accounting research memoranda. The chapter concludes with writing strategies, including how to effectively reference authoritative guidance, and style tips for professional communication. To bring all of these ideas together, the chapter appendix includes a sample issues memo.

It's quite common for beginning researchers to view documentation style as an area of personal preference, or as an area where instructors nitpick needlessly. "This isn't an English class!" is a comment that accounting research instructors have come to dread. I urge you to approach this chapter with an open mind. The more effectively you can communicate your research, the more you'll be seen as an effective researcher. The tips outlined in this chapter are intended to help you communicate in the style used by technical accountants in our field, from junior staff to national offices.

DOCUMENTATION IS INTEGRAL TO ACCOUNTING RESEARCH

LO1 Explain the importance of documentation.

Recall from previous chapters that the objectives of accounting research are generally twofold:

1. To account for transactions or items in a manner that is appropriate and **supportable** based on authoritative guidance, and
2. To create **documentation** describing the research performed and supporting the conclusion reached.

In other words, *performing* accounting research is only half the battle. You must also clearly *document* your research. Accounting research involves **professional judgment**. The best way to support the judgments you are making is through thoughtful documentation.

Documentation is critical to accounting research because

- The exercise itself of creating documentation can cause you to think through accounting issues more critically than if you simply discuss the issues.

- Creating documentation of the basis for accounting positions creates an audit trail. Not only will the files be useful for historical reference, but current documentation can be shared with the company's auditors, helping the auditors understand and review the company's accounting judgments in real time.

- This transaction sets precedent for future transactions. Without proper documentation, company accountants could risk reaching a different conclusion if this type of transaction is later repeated. This could result in inconsistent accounting or, worse, restatement if company accountants conclude that the prior transaction's accounting is improper and the transaction is material.

- If your company's accounting position on a transaction is ever questioned (for example, through an SEC comment letter, in the event of a lawsuit, or by regulators), ideally, your company's rationale for the accounting would already be neatly summarized into a memo. In theory, that memo could be forwarded straight over to the SEC in response to their inquiry.

- Auditors must also maintain documentation evidencing their reviews of judgmental client accounting positions. This documentation shows that the auditor was diligent in researching and evaluating whether client positions are appropriate.

Furthermore, know that when you create robust documentation, you protect yourself—in a sense—from the sort of "hindsight bias" that we read about in Chapter 2. The following comments from the SEC staff, which emphasize the importance of robust, timely documentation to support judgments, further illustrate this point:

> "The alternatives considered and the conclusions reached should be documented contemporaneously. This will ensure that the evaluation of the judgment is based on the same facts that were reasonably available at the time the judgment was made . . ."[1]

By walking your reader through your analysis, in real time as you make accounting judgments, you demonstrate to the reader that your process for evaluating the issue was robust and appropriate in light of facts known at the time.

Remember that it's often your end product—your research report—which determines whether your research is seen as high-quality. Understanding the importance of writing skills, this chapter walks you through not only the form and content of professional accounting docu-

---

[1] Final Report of the Advisory Committee on Improvements to Financial Reporting to the United States Securities and Exchange Commission, August 1, 2008. Page 96.

mentation, but also some of the finer points to writing in a style that will impress even the most technical of accountants.

COMMUNICATING ACCOUNTING RESEARCH

Let's take a closer look at how to communicate the results of your research. We will explore two common methods for communicating accounting research:

- Emails
- Accounting issues memoranda

Notably, client letters are another form of communicating accounting research, but are not a focus of this chapter.

One overarching tip, as we move into our discussion of writing: *Know your audience.* Start out any writing assignment by considering who will read your work, then write at a level that your reader will understand.

For example, the level of detail you provide in your Codification references (**ASC 842**, versus "the Leases topic") may depend upon whether you are writing to a technical accountant, versus a member of the Finance team at your company.

In his Preface to the SEC's Plain English Handbook, Warren Buffett offers the following suggestion:

> One unoriginal but useful tip: Write with a specific person in mind. When writing Berkshire Hathaway's annual report, I pretend that I'm talking to my sisters. I have no trouble picturing them: Though highly intelligent, they are not experts in accounting or finance. They will understand plain English, but jargon may puzzle them. My goal is simply to give them the information I would wish them to supply me if our positions were reversed. To succeed, I don't need to be Shakespeare; I must, though, have a sincere desire to inform.[2]

In many cases, your audience for accounting research communications will be your supervisor, your auditors, and—possibly—regulators who might later scrutinize a transaction. Accordingly, much of the accounting research communication that we will cover in this chapter will be written to an audience of fellow accountants. However, it's important in all cases to consider your audience before you begin writing.

Let's look now at how to write professional emails.

EMAILING THE RESULTS OF RESEARCH QUESTIONS

Email is often useful for communicating the results of limited-scope research questions. This is often the case when you are not the "owner" of the issue (i.e., the party responsible for documenting or concluding on the complete issue), but rather are helping provide relevant guidance to some aspect of an issue that a colleague is managing.

LO2 Draft effective emails to communicate the results of limited-scope research.

Here is an example of a professional email responding to a limited-scope research question. In this example, Jenn, a staff member at Presto Hospitality, has been asked to help Michael research whether the stadium owner has a *substantive right of substitution* with respect to the portable concession spaces that Presto has the right to use in the agreement. As you may recall, understanding whether the supplier has a substantive right of substitution is critical to understanding whether the arrangement involves *identified* property, plant, or equipment. Jenn's response is as follows:

---

[2] Office of Investor Education and Assistance, of the U.S. Securities and Exchange Commission. *A Plain English Handbook: How to create clear SEC disclosure documents.* 1998. Preface.

Re: Stadium Co.'s substitution rights (portables)

Michael,

You asked me to research whether Stadium Co. has a substantive right of substitution with respect to the portables in the draft concessions contract. Based on the following guidance, I have concluded that Stadium Co. *does* have a substantive right of substitution, and thus the portables would not be considered identified assets (even if their locations are initially specified in the contract).

Per ASC 842-10:

15-10   Even if an asset is specified, a customer does not have the right to use an identified asset if the supplier has the substantive right to substitute the asset throughout the period of use. A supplier's right to substitute an asset is substantive only if **both** . . . :

a.   The supplier has the practical ability to substitute alternative assets throughout the period of use (for example, the customer cannot prevent the supplier from substituting an asset, and alternative assets are readily available to the supplier or could be sourced by the supplier within a reasonable period of time).

b.   The supplier would benefit economically from the exercise of its right to substitute the asset (that is, the economic benefits associated with substituting the asset are expected to exceed the costs associated with substituting the asset). [Emphasis added]

Implementation guidance in ASC 842-10 provides an example involving airport concession space that is similar to the portable carts in our arrangement:

> > > Example 2—Concession Space

55-52   A coffee company (Customer) enters into a contract with an airport operator (Supplier) to use a space in the airport to sell its goods for a three-year period. The contract states the amount of space and that the space may be located at any one of several boarding areas within the airport. Supplier has the right to change the location of the space allocated to Customer at any time during the period of use. There are minimal costs to Supplier associated with changing the space for the Customer: Customer uses a kiosk (that it owns) that can be moved easily to sell its goods. There are many areas in the airport that are available and that would meet the specifications for the space in the contract.

55-53   The contract does not contain a lease.

55-54   Although the amount of space Customer uses is specified in the contract, there is no identified asset. ...[T]he contract is for space in the airport, and this space can change at the discretion of Supplier. Supplier has the substantive right to substitute the space Customer uses because:

a.   Supplier has the practical ability to change the space used by Customer throughout the period of use. There are many areas in the airport that meet the specifications for the space in the contract, and Supplier has the right to change the location of the space to other space that meets the specifications at any time without Customer's approval.

b.   Supplier would benefit economically from substituting the space. There would be minimal cost associated with changing the space used by Customer because the kiosk can be moved easily. Supplier benefits from substituting the space in the airport because substitution allows Supplier to make the most effective use of the space at boarding areas in the airport to meet changing circumstances.

Continued

Continued from previous page

> In our case, like this airport kiosk example, Stadium Co.: a) has the contractual right to substitute the location of the portables and has access to alternate spaces that could be used; and b) would incur only minimal (if any) cost in substituting the space. Therefore, this substitution right is substantive.
>
> This analysis may be less clear when performed for fixed concession stands, which could involve additional supplier cost to substitute. Let me know if you'd like me to research that issue next.
>
> Thanks for letting me assist with this question.
>
> Jenn

The sample email above exhibits qualities that you should generally try to include in your professional email communications. Here are some of the lessons learned from this email:

- Keep it brief. The sample email above is concise, yet complete in its response to the question.

- Include a subject line that briefly describes the accounting issue you've researched, and the client name.

- Re-state the question: "You asked me to research . . ."

- Include an excerpt from authoritative guidance to support your response.

- Use complete sentences.

- If you made any assumptions in researching the issue, state what you assumed. It's likely that you will have to make assumptions if you have only limited background on an issue.

- Reread, possibly print, the email before you send it. This will help you identify confusing or weak language, as well as grammatical errors.

- Do not say "I think/feel"; this isn't about you. It's about what guidance is on point. If you are unsure about how guidance should be read, you can say: "It appears . . ."

- Avoid exclamation points, in order to keep your tone as professional as possible.

- Include an offer to be of further assistance.

One of my former **accounting research** colleagues made it a habit to print and reread *every* substantive email to a client or supervisor before sending it. She wanted to always put her most professional self forward. Her thoughtful approach to research—combined with her attention to detail—has paid dividends for her career; she went on to work in the SEC's Office of the Chief Accountant and currently is a partner in the national office of a major firm.

[**TIP**] from the Trenches

Drafting a Professional Email

You are a staff auditor reviewing the Statement of Cash Flows for Auto Corp (the client). The senior on your audit team (Robin) has asked you to research whether the client has appropriately classified the proceeds from the sale of its manufacturing facility as cash flows from investing activities.

Draft an email response to Robin's question. Use the Codification guidance in Figure 3-1 to support your response.

Now
[**YOU**]
Try
3.1

> **Classification**

45-10   A statement of cash flows shall classify cash receipts and cash payments as resulting from investing, financing, or operating activities.

> > **Cash Flows from Investing Activities**

45-11   Cash flows from purchases, sales, and maturities of available-for-sale debt securities shall be classified as cash flows from **investing activities** and reported gross in the statement of cash flows.

45-12   All of the following are cash inflows from investing activities:

a. Receipts from collections or sales of loans made by the entity and of other entities' debt instruments (other than cash equivalents, certain debt instruments that are acquired specifically for resale . . . , and certain donated debt instruments received by not-for-profit entities (NFPs) . . .)

b. Receipts from sales of equity instruments of other entities . . . and from returns of investment in those instruments

c. Receipts from sales of property, plant, and equipment and other productive assets . . .

Reproduced with permission of the Financial Accounting Foundation.

Your response here _____
_____
_____
_____
_____
_____
_____
_____
_____
_____
_____
_____
_____
_____
_____

[**TIP**] from the
Trenches

A final tip on the subject of emails . . . Ever wonder if sending a higher-ranking colleague a quick "thank you" email, after they have assisted you, will bother them? As a young professional, I recall wondering the same thing.

But trust me, a quick "Thanks for your help!" note is never a bother to receive. These emails are a win-win: You're showing that you're a grateful, appreciative person, and the note will make your colleague or instructor smile (and can be easily deleted—it's really not a nuisance).

As a general rule of thumb, if someone assists you, don't second guess it. Send a quick thanks.

DRAFTING AN ACCOUNTING ISSUES MEMORANDUM

Documentation in the form of an accounting issues memorandum is generally warranted when a transaction is complex, judgmental, or highly material. Each company should have policies in place for when such documentation is required, and at what point in the transaction review process. It is considered a best practice to evaluate and document the accounting for a transaction at or before the time the transaction is executed. In certain cases, such "contemporaneous" documentation is *required*.

Accounting issues memos are often organized into sections similar to those presented in Figure 3-2. Of course, this format is subject to some variation by company; for example, some companies prefer to include an Executive Summary section at the beginning of the issues memo. Nevertheless, we'll refer to the layout presented in Figure 3-2 as the **standard memo format**.

Figure 3-2

Standard memo format

Facts
State the relevant facts surrounding the issue.
Often, drawing a picture is helpful.

Issues
List the researchable questions you're trying to answer.

Analysis
Include all relevant authoritative guidance, along with analysis in your own words of how the guidance applies to your fact pattern.

Conclusion
State your conclusion based on your research findings, highlighting key factors considered.
Provide additional discussion for highly judgmental issues.

Financial Statement and Disclosure Impacts
Summarize financial statement accounts affected and any disclosures required.
Include journal entries when possible.

The issues memorandum should include all of the sections shown in Figure 3-2. Present these section headers in bold to improve the readability of your memo. A sample accounting issues memo, which addresses the Presto Hospitality concessions agreement, is included in an Appendix at the end of this chapter.

Your ultimate goal with the issues memo is to create a "one-stop shop" for knowledge about this transaction and its accounting. A reader, after picking up your memo, should not have to do additional digging to fully understand the background or the support for the accounting conclusion. After reading your memo, if a reader finds it necessary to get additional key facts from the contract, or to read additional guidance from the Codification, then you have failed to make your memo a one-stop shop.

TIP from the Trenches

Facts

LO3 **Formulate** an effective Facts section and Issues list in an accounting research memo.

The Facts (or Background) section of an issues memo should include *all relevant background* necessary for understanding the transaction and its accounting. This section should be concise, but not sparse. Aim to provide enough detail about the issue that a party uninvolved with the matter could pick up the memo—even years later—and understand the issue well enough to form an opinion as to whether or not the accounting treatment is appropriate.

Step 1 of the research process, described in the preceding chapter, outlines the **process** necessary to understand the facts and background of a transaction. Relevant information obtained from this step 1 should be included in the Facts section of an issues memo.

Transactions are often complex. A *picture of a transaction*, included within the Facts section of a memo, can greatly enhance a reader's understanding of the relationships and parties involved in the issue. These can be fairly easy to create using the "shapes" feature in Word. In the picture, try to show as much information about the relationships among the parties as you can (parent/subsidiary relationships, what each party gives or gets from the other, etc.).[3]

For example, here is a simple picture for the following arrangement:

- Two unrelated entities are entering into a joint venture (JV). Entity A contributes $1,000 to the JV for 50% of the equity ownership, and Entity B makes a $2,000 loan to the JV for 50% of the ownership.

Figure 3-3

Picture of joint venture arrangement

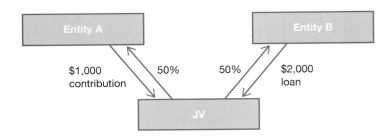

Notice how, just by looking at the picture in Figure 3-3, you can get a basic understanding of the relationships between the parties. To illustrate a slightly more complex arrangement, let's add new facts to this example. Let's assume that Entity A is owned by Entity 1, and assume that Entity B is owned by Entity 2. Let's also assume that a bank loans the JV $500. Often when drawing a picture, ownership can be implied by a vertical relationship between two entities.

Figure 3-4

Picture of joint venture with ownership by Entities 1 and 2

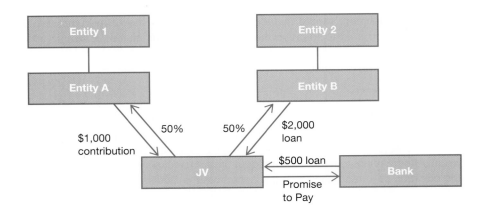

---

[3] The relationship between the parties in the Presto Hospitality transaction is fairly straightforward; accordingly, the Ch. 3 Appendix sample memo does not include a picture.

Notice a few things about the picture in Figure 3-4. First, even without "100%" written next to the line connecting Entity 1 and Entity A, the vertical relationship implies full ownership. Second, as the bank is not involved as an owner, it is not drawn in a vertical relationship; it is shown to the side of the JV to indicate that it is an outside, third party.

There is no magic to drawing a picture for inclusion in a memo. The idea is just to portray relationships in a way that readers can easily understand.

Drawing a Picture

Now
YOU
Try
3.2

Draw a picture for the following arrangement:

- Entity A owns Entity B and Entity C. Entities B and C enter into a joint venture ("the JV"). Entity B contributes $20,000 for 99% of the equity ownership. Entity C contributes $500 for 1% of the equity and will serve as manager of the JV. Bank lends the JV $1 million.

- Hint: Beside the line representing Entity C's contribution of $500, you can also write "manager," as this is a type of service that Entity C is contributing to the JV.

Your picture here

The approach for drawing pictures outlined in this chapter came from what I learned in the field, informally. My colleagues at the FASB used to sketch out transaction structure pictures on whiteboards—just to facilitate conversations we had amongst ourselves, and that practice continued in my roles in advisory and corporate accounting. More formal diagramming methods exist but are not covered in this guide.[3]

TIP from the Trenches

Finally, it is often helpful at the end of the Facts section to very briefly (1–2 sentences) set up the overall issue to be addressed. That is, you're not listing out your research questions yet, but you can set the stage for the overall themes that you plan to address in the memo.

For example: Presto must determine whether this arrangement contains a lease within the scope of ASC 842 (Leases).

Beginning researchers often struggle with wording when setting the stage. Avoid statements such as:

- Presto *must choose* how to record this transaction. Or,
- Presto *has the option* to record this arrangement as a lease.

Rather than describing an accounting policy determination as a *choice* or an *option*, think of Presto's objective as to *determine* which accounting method is *most appropriate*. Or, to determine *whether it should* account for the transaction as a lease.

Issue(s)

The Issues (or Questions) section of the memo should follow immediately after the Facts section. Under the header "Issue(s)," list your researchable question(s). Often, there may be multiple questions to address. For example, let's assume that your company (Manufacturer Co.) recently contributed assets to form a joint venture (JV) with another company. To evaluate the accounting for this arrangement, your memo could list the following research questions:

Issues:

1. Is Manufacturer required to consolidate the JV?
2. If consolidation is not required, how should Manufacturer account for its investment in the JV?
3. How will Manufacturer record its asset contribution to the JV?

Notice that each issue is phrased in the form of a question, and these research questions should be listed together at the beginning of the memo (in the Issues section). It's often the case with complex issues (as is the case here) that each research question builds on the previous question. Had this been a simpler topic, a single issue ("Issue 1") might suffice to determine the accounting, and a second issue ("Issue 2") might address required disclosures.

There is no magic to picking the perfect research questions. In fact, in this scenario, you might have chosen to break Issue 1 down into several issues, such as:

1. Is the joint venture within the scope of the variable interest entity (VIE) accounting model?
2. If not, how should Manufacturer apply the voting model to this arrangement?

Or, more detailed still: *Does Manufacturer have a variable interest in the joint venture? Does the joint venture qualify for a scope exception to the VIE model?*, and so on.

In short, the goal in selecting issues is to organize your accounting analysis in a logical way, which clearly walks your reader through the issues you faced and the research you performed. Use your judgment as to how best to organize your issues.

[**TIP**] from the Trenches

As an accounting research instructor, I often assign case studies that have questions intended to guide the students in addressing all key issues. A common mistake students make is to organize their memo entirely based on these discussion questions, exactly as provided.

But the thing is, *you*—as writer—are responsible for deciding how to organize your memo in a manner that most clearly introduces the topic and walks readers through the relevant issues. This all starts with how you organize the issues list. Don't assume this list should be an exact match to the discussion questions provided.

Analysis

LO4 Prepare an effective research analysis, including consideration of alternative viewpoints, and a well-supported conclusion.

The Analysis section is arguably the most critical component of a well-written issues memo. In this section, you will address each issue listed, one at a time. In our Presto Hospitality example, Michael might title the first Analysis section, for example, **Analysis of Issue 1:** *Does the Concessions Agreement involve an identified asset?*

Tying Together the Guidance and Case Facts

The Analysis section is aptly named because in it you will include *excerpts* from authoritative guidance, along with *commentary* in your own words about how the guidance applies to your transaction. Nonauthoritative guidance may also be included in this section of your memo, as a supplement to authoritative guidance.

A leading professor in accounting research described a common student struggle with the analysis section, as follows:

The Analysis section is really the key and what I often find most lacking in students' reports. That's because they don't do a good job of reasoning from the facts of the case, using the literature they found, to reach the appropriate conclusion. Rather, their process is more like: here are the facts, here is research, here is a conclusion.

In other words, the analysis section is your chance to bring together the facts of the case, the literature, and your evaluation of judgments or alternatives in the guidance. You must take the time to really *relate the guidance to your specific fact pattern*. Pull in actual words from your summary of the facts, and describe how they relate to actual words from the guidance.

As an example, consider the following excerpt from Michael's analysis of Presto's concessions agreement. In this excerpt, Michael is reviewing **ASC 842-10** (Leases) to determine whether a portion of an asset (such as the right to use parts of a stadium) can be the subject of a lease. Notice how Michael's analysis brings together authoritative guidance and the facts of this arrangement.

EXAMPLE ───

Par. 15-16 provides the following guidance regarding whether a portion of an asset is an identified asset:

> > > Portions of Assets

15-16 A capacity portion of an asset is an identified asset if it is **physically distinct** (for example, a floor of a building or a segment of a pipeline that connects a single customer to the larger pipeline). A capacity or other portion of an asset that is not physically distinct (for example, a capacity portion of a fiber optic cable) is not an identified asset, unless it represents substantially all of the capacity of the asset and thereby provides the customer with the right to obtain substantially all of the economic benefits from use of the asset. [Emphasis added]

As the Food and Beverage Facilities represent a portion of a broader asset (the Stadium), these facilities are only considered an *identified asset* if they are *physically distinct*.

In this arrangement, certain of the Food and Beverage Facilities (specifically, fixed concession stands) are specified on architectural drawings and are thus physically distinct. Additionally, the right to serve food and beverages in premium seating areas, including suites, involves physically distinct spaces. These concession stands and premium areas can be used independently from one another. Therefore, these spaces are all considered *physically distinct.*

By contrast, other rights in the contract, such as the right to operate portables and the right to have food and beverage hawkers operating throughout the stadium, do not involve physically distinct portions of an asset. The location of the portable carts is not specified, and therefore any location within the stadium could be used to locate the carts. Per par. 15-16, if a portion of an asset is not physically distinct, it "is not an identified asset, unless it represents substantially all of the capacity of the asset…". This condition is not present, as use of the portables and rights of the hawkers within the broader Stadium do not represent "substantially all" of the Stadium's capacity. Therefore, these rights do not involve identified assets.

Did you notice in Michael's analysis that he discussed how the guidance relates specifically to Presto's fact pattern? See how he says: "In this arrangement, certain of the Food and Beverage Facilities . . . are specified on architectural drawings and are thus physically distinct." He is walking us through his *reasoning*, as opposed to simply stating: *This arrangement involves identified assets.*

Present Available Alternatives

Recall that the analysis section should clearly describe any alternatives available in accounting for a given transaction, weighing their relative merits. Remember that accounting research isn't always just about the destination; *how you get* to a particular accounting treatment matters too. I don't accept the argument from students that the only goal is to get to the right answer. Rather, the analysis section is your opportunity to walk the reader through your thought process. What guidance did you consider? What alternatives were present? Was application of the guidance judgmental? Could other guidance have applied?

There is an old saying among auditors that **"If it wasn't documented, it wasn't done."** Even if you as a researcher consider other alternatives to the conclusion reached, if these alternatives are not documented, there is no evidence that you did so. Should your judgments ever be challenged, it becomes much more difficult to demonstrate the thoroughness of your work if the alternatives considered were not documented at the time of evaluation.

Considering Michael's case, it would not have been enough for him to assume that the arrangement involves identified assets and to go straight to the next step of the lease evaluation. Even though the end result may be the same, Michael must walk his readers through his evaluation, demonstrating how he determined which rights in the agreement are considered *identified assets*.

Furthermore, by presenting available alternatives in your memo, you are being upfront with your reader. You are showing the reader that your conclusion involved judgment. This is a good thing. To illustrate this point, consider the following TIP from the Trenches.

[TIP] from the Trenches

The only way someone reading your documentation will trust your conclusion is if you have clearly identified the available alternatives in your analysis.

In the past, I have asked students to document the accounting required for a certain transaction, knowing that when they began to explore the guidance, they would be presented with two alternatives.

- The "A" papers are the ones where students say: "Two alternatives exist (method A and method B). Method A appears to be more appropriate for this situation because . . ."

- The "B" or "C" papers are the ones where students say: "Method A should be followed because . . ." without mentioning that an alternative treatment is available.

As an employer, I would place more trust in the work of the "A" students. Even if I disagree with their choice of accounting method, at least I have been made aware that two choices exist. In contrast, the "B" or "C" papers did not give me the full story. When reviewing future submissions from these "employees," I would likely perform the extra step of rechecking the guidance they cite for completeness.

Tips for Incorporating Guidance—the Guidance Sandwich

Recall the "one-stop shop" concept described earlier. Your Analysis section should include enough excerpts from the authoritative guidance that a reader will not have to go back to the Codification (or other applicable authority) in order to understand the support for your analysis. Don't just refer generally to the guidance, or paraphrase the guidance into your own words. Rather, include enough actual excerpts to clearly make your case, then analyze this guidance in your own words.

As a general rule of thumb, your own commentary should *precede and follow* all guidance excerpts.

Ever heard of the interpersonal communication concept of a "compliment sandwich"? It goes something like this: If you're going to criticize someone, say something nice before and after the criticism. For example, "Joe, I like your tie today. I really wish you would do something about your bad breath. By the way, nice job on that report."

Think of your analysis section as a series of *guidance sandwiches*, with your own words introducing, and then analyzing each guidance excerpt.

EXAMPLE ———————————————————————————————————

Following is a simple guidance sandwich that illustrates Michael's initial consideration of the guidance regarding whether a contract contains an identified asset.

Identified Asset

ASC 842-10 states the following with respect to determining whether a contract involves an *identified asset:*

> 15-9 An asset typically is identified by being explicitly specified in a contract. However, an asset also can be identified by being implicitly specified at the time that the asset is made available for use by the customer.

The baseball stadium (an asset) is explicitly specified in the contract. However, Presto only has the right to use specified portions of the stadium. Accordingly, two challenges that arise in applying the concept of *identified asset* to this agreement include evaluating 1) when a *portion of an asset* is an identified asset and 2) whether the supplier has a *substantive right to substitute* the asset.

Notice how the example provides commentary in Michael's own words before and after the guidance excerpt. The first sentence of the example introduces the guidance and states why it is being considered. The quote from the guidance is inserted next. Finally, the last sentence applies the guidance to the company's own set of facts.

Nonauthoritative sources that you consider would be presented in a similar manner, following the authoritative sources you present.

In the commentary that follows guidance excerpts, incorporate key words considered from the guidance. Don't be creative in re-stating guidance requirements. Rather, use the words that were just provided to you, so as to avoid inadvertently changing the meaning of the guidance.

Take a moment now to identify the guidance sandwich you used in the email example earlier in this chapter.

Guidance Sandwiches

Remember the email you drafted to your audit senior (Robin) regarding the Statement of Cash Flows for Auto Corp? Take a moment now to identify the guidance sandwich you used in that email (or, take a moment to create one now). Recall that you are responding to Robin's question about whether the client has appropriately classified the proceeds from the sale of its manufacturing facility as cash flows from investing activities.

Hint: Your guidance sandwich could start with, for example:

▦ **ASC xxx states that cash flows from investing activities include . . . "(x)."**

Your response here _____

_____

_____

_____

_____

Now
YOU
Try
3.3

Next, let's focus on how to organize your analysis.

Organizing Your Analysis

Use additional *subheaders* throughout your analysis, as needed to help guide your reader. For example, in Michael's memo evaluating Presto's concessions agreement, he uses the following subheader to help guide readers through his evaluation of Issue 1.

> **Analysis—Issue 1: Does the Concessions Agreement involve an *identified asset*?**
> *Portion of an Asset*
> *Substantive Right to Substitute*
> - Practical Ability to Substitute
> - Economically would benefit from substitution

Notice how Michael uses subheaders to clearly organize his analysis of the identified asset requirements (namely, *portion of an asset, and substantive right to substitute*). Use of subheaders can be valuable for organizing your analysis of guidance with multiple conditions. Of course, you might choose to break this single "Issue 1" down into multiple issues, or researchable questions. Refer to the Appendix to see how Michael used these subheaders to organize his Issue 1 analysis.

In some cases, you will encounter guidance with multiple conditions, often shown as "and" or "or" conditions. Generally speaking, "and" conditions must all be met in order for a certain accounting treatment to apply. With "or" conditions, only one condition must be met.

In such cases (both for "and" or "or"), it is a best practice to evaluate each condition provided. Take, for example, the definition of a derivative. For a contract to meet the definition of a derivative, it must: 1) have a notional and an underlying (e.g., a quantity and a price); *and* 2) require little/no initial net investment; *and* 3) be capable of net settlement. A researcher in this case might organize his or her analysis as follows:

ASC 815-10 (Derivatives) defines derivative instruments as follows:

[Guidance Excerpt]—Par. 15-83 (Definition of a derivative instrument)

The company has analyzed each characteristic, as follows.

Characteristic 1 - The contract has both an underlying and a notional amount.
Analysis:

Characteristic 2 - The contract requires no initial net investment.
Analysis:

Characteristic 3 - The contract can be settled net.
Analysis:

In this example, the full guidance excerpt is presented, followed by analysis of each required characteristic. Notice how the use of these subheaders improves the readability of the analysis.

Now YOU Try 3.4

Assume you are preparing a memo to evaluate whether a lease should receive operating or finance treatment. Five conditions are provided; if any one condition is met, the lease should be classified as a finance lease. Assume the first condition (transfer of ownership) is met. Should you still evaluate the remaining four conditions? Explain.

_____

_____

Could subheaders be used to organize your analysis of the lease criteria? Explain.

_____

Consider Including Journal Entries for Each Alternative

To the extent you are weighing alternative accounting treatments, consider including (in your Analysis section) the journal entries that would apply to each alternative. Identifying the impact each alternative will have on the financial statements can help you recognize a client's motivation for a particular accounting treatment (e.g., income manipulation). Also, seeing how alternative treatments would play out on the financial statements can help researchers visually connect the substance of a transaction to its possible financial statement impacts.

You won't always find journal entry guidance in the Codification, so you'll often need to think through this part of the analysis on your own, or by considering other sources.

Document Other Factors Considered

Finally, in addition to analyzing the requirements of accounting guidance (both from authoritative and nonauthoritative sources), the Analysis section of an issues memo is also the appropriate place for discussion of other key factors considered in determining an appropriate accounting treatment.

For example:

- How are peer companies accounting for this type of transaction?
- How has our company handled this type of transaction historically?
- Did we consult with subject-matter experts in analyzing this issue?

Present your consideration of these other factors, as applicable, following your review of authoritative literature.

Flip back to the par. 15-16 example presented earlier, and respond to the following.

1. First, label the guidance sandwich shown in that example. Use the following labels: 1. Introduction in the author's own words. 2. Guidance excerpt. 3. Commentary in author's own words.

2. Next, in the author's commentary (which follows the guidance excerpt), underline any words that the author repeated from the guidance.

3. What might be a benefit of restating parts of the guidance when performing your analysis?

_____

_____

4. Circle places where the author discusses the case facts, and how they relate to the guidance.

5. Why is it important to discuss case facts in your analysis of guidance excerpts?

_____

_____

Now
YOU
Try
3.5

Conclusion

Complete your discussion of each separate issue with a clearly written **conclusion**. This section should briefly summarize key points from your analysis that were considered in arriving at the conclusion reached.

Once you reach the point of documenting your conclusion, in many cases it may already be fairly obvious from your analysis which treatment is most appropriate. In such cases, your conclusion can be fairly brief. For example, following is Michael's conclusion section documenting his determination that the rights to operate fixed concession stands and to serve in premium seating areas involve *identified assets*.

> **Conclusion—Issue 1: Identified Asset**
>
> The Food and Beverage Facilities are a portion of an asset, and thus these spaces are considered "identified assets" if they are physically distinct and not subject to substantive substitution rights. We have concluded the following:
>
> - Fixed concession stands, suites, and premium areas are physically distinct and are not subject to a substantive substitution right (given that relocation would be costly and thus unlikely). These locations are considered identified assets.
> - With respect to the right for hawkers to operate in the stadium, the hawkers are not limited to a defined space (i.e., the space is not physically distinct), and thus this right does not involve an identified asset.
> - With respect to portables, the locations are not physically distinct, *and* Stadium Co. has a substantive right of substitution. Thus, portables are not considered *identified assets.*
>
> Therefore, the identified assets in this arrangement are 1) fixed concession stands and 2) premium seating areas and suites.

Now
[YOU]
Try
3.6

What are some of the factors that Michael pointed to when describing how he reached the conclusion that portable concession stands are not identified assets?

_____

_____

_____

Notice that, even in this example of a brief conclusion, the author summarized the most compelling points in the analysis as support for the conclusion. It is not sufficient to say:

In conclusion, portables are not identified assets.

Rather, the following underlined text should be added to such a conclusion, restating the rationale for the conclusion:

In conclusion, <u>because of factors x, y, and z,</u> portables are not considered identified assets.

[TIP] from the Trenches

Don't "jump to" conclusions. Make sure your conclusion includes your rationale (for example, "because of factors x, y, and z"), rather than simply naming the alternative selected.

In cases where the choice between two or more alternatives is highly judgmental, the conclusion should be longer and more detailed. The conclusion should clearly explain which requirements from the guidance, along with other factors considered, were compelling in selecting an alternative. The researcher might comment on why the alternative selected best reflects the substance and business purpose of the transaction. The rationale articulated in the conclusion could later become a critical part of the audit trail if the accounting for the transaction is ever called into question. That said, do not introduce new arguments in your conclusion. Rather, all relevant factors should be introduced in your Analysis, and then the most key factors should be discussed and referred back to in the conclusion.

TIP | from the Trenches

Should you use one Conclusion section, or several, in a memo with multiple issues?
    It depends on the complexity of the issues you've analyzed. If the issues are straightforward and your analysis is fairly brief, one Conclusion section may be sufficient. However, when addressing more complex issues, each issue may require its own Conclusion section.

Financial Statement and Disclosure Impacts

When applicable, conclude your memo with a summary of **financial statement and disclosure impacts**. Journal entries can be useful in describing anticipated financial statement impacts.

Continue to use the same writing process and format, such as citing authoritative guidance as support, in writing this section. In other words, show the journal entries that will be required based on your conclusion. If you are able to find authoritative excerpts that support either side of the entry (debits or credits), then include that guidance as support for the entry. As noted previously, journal entry guidance is often not provided in the Codification; to the extent you refer to other sources for journal entry guidance, you should include a reference to those sources.

For disclosures, include authoritative excerpts describing disclosure requirements, followed by discussion of how the company will comply with these requirements, specifically to address this issue.

Reread Your Work Before Submitting (and what to look for)

By now, you've prepared a thoughtful, complete accounting analysis. But is it ready to send to your supervisor?

Always reread your work before submitting. Check for:

- Commas, spelling, and proper grammar (more on this in a moment)
- Consistent font (generally, go with 11–12 point, Times, single spaced but double space between paragraphs)
- Concise, clear sentences
- Active voice

In other words, this reread process is your chance to fine-tune your writing. Doing so will give your paper extra polish, and will add that "wow" factor (what a professional, strong writer!).

TIP | from the Trenches

Writing an issues memo may require three passes. On your first pass, get your rough draft thoughts down and the technical details in place. On your second pass, reread your work, adjusting the order of sentences and paragraphs as necessary to organize your thoughts in a more logical manner. Also, use this review to strengthen, or beef up, your arguments as needed. On your final pass, review your wording for opportunities to communicate more clearly and directly.

Concise, Clear Sentences

Recognizing that technical accounting is challenging to communicate, the SEC released a *Plain English Handbook* in 1998. In it, the SEC encourages companies to prepare disclosure documents that investors can easily understand, and offers strategies to that effect (Write in active voice! Use clear section headings! Know your audience! Be concise!). The handbook states: "A plain English document uses words economically and at a level the audience can understand. Its sentence structure is tight."[4]

---

[4] Office of Investor Education and Assistance, of the U.S. Securities and Exchange Commission. *A Plain English Handbook: How to create clear SEC disclosure documents.* 1998. Page 5.

In reviewing your own work for clear and concise wording, ask yourself: Can I rephrase any of my sentences to be more concise? Can I eliminate unnecessary words?

Active Voice

Your writing will generally be clearer, and more direct, if you write in active voice. Consider the following examples of active vs. passive voice.

> The girl was bitten by the dog.   (Passive voice)
>
> The dog bit the girl.   (Active Voice)

In active voice, the subject performs the action described by the verb. For clarity, keep the subject and verb close together.

[Now
YOU
Try
3.7]

Change the following sentence to active voice, and see if you can word it more concisely.

> The documentation put together by you should be carefully subjected to an editing process.

_____

_____

[**TIP** | from the
Trenches]

While the research you submit should always be your own effort, you might consider having a reviewer proofread your writing. Especially if you struggle in this area, a trusted peer, or the school's writing center, can offer comments on your grammar and spelling. Have your reviewers hand-write their comments, so you can input and learn from their edits.

PROPERLY REFERENCING ACCOUNTING GUIDANCE

[**LO5** | Properly refer-
ence passages
from the Codification.]

How Do I Reference a Passage from the Codification?

Excerpts from authoritative guidance are critical to effective accounting research communications. Paraphrasing guidance (that is, summarizing it into your own words) is not enough; authoritative guidance is far more impactful in a memo than a summary of guidance in your own words. Additionally, quoting "Codification excerpts" from articles or textbooks is inappropriate; always get authoritative guidance directly from the Codification. This discussion focuses on how to properly cite guidance excerpts from the Codification.

The first time you refer to the Codification in a memo, give its full title ("FASB Accounting Standards Codification"). Include the numerical reference for the topic you are citing, as well as a parenthetical description of the topic name. For example:

■ Per FASB Accounting Standards Codification (**ASC**) topic **360-10-35-1** (Property, Plant, and Equipment), . . .

Remember that not everyone reading your memo was an accounting major and understands the acronym **ASC**. Therefore, it is important initially to provide the full name of the Codification, then to use the parenthetical (**ASC**) to show that you will abbreviate this term in future references within the memo.

After your initial reference to the Codification, it is acceptable to refer to the topic using the abbreviation "**ASC**," and omitting the parenthetical topic name (Property, Plant, and Equipment). For example,

■ Per **ASC 360-10-35-2**: . . .

Note how these sample numerical references go all the way down to the paragraph level. Always provide as much detail as possible. Your reference would be lacking if you sent readers to Topic **360-10**, as that leaves them with pages of guidance to sort through to find what you are trying to reference. Do your readers the favor of getting them directly to the appropriate paragraph within the guidance.

In citing guidance, don't get creative with sentence structure. Following are examples of both strong and weak references. Stick to the strong references, and your memos will have a more professional tone.

- Strong references:
  - According to **ASC xxx**, "Quote"
  - **ASC xxx** states or **ASC xxx** requires: "Quote"
  - Per **ASC xxx**: "Quote"
  - **ASC xxx** provides the following guidance: "Quote"
  - The rate of return shall be based on: "Quote" (**ASC xxx**).
  - The rate of return shall be based on: "Quote" [fn 1]
    (at end of page) Footnote 1: **ASC xxx**

- Weak references:
  - **ASC xxx** asks readers to . . . "Quote"
  - **ASC xxx** believes . . . "Quote"
  - The Codification writes . . . "Quote" (**ASC xxx**)
  - The FASB says . . . "Quote" (**ASC xxx**)
  - I found the following guidance . . . "Quote" (**ASC xxx**)

Take careful note of the language and punctuation used in the preceding examples. "Per **ASC xxx**" is followed by a colon (:). "According to **ASC xxx**" is followed by a comma (,). All of the lead-ins just listed should be followed by excerpts from the guidance. Additionally, each excerpt includes a reference to the source of the guidance (**ASC xxx**). Note that these numerical references should get down to the paragraph-level of detail, since each provides a quotation directly from a paragraph of the guidance.

Referencing the Codification

Fill in the blanks using strong reference words.

1. _____ **ASC 360-10-35-17**, "An impairment loss shall be recognized only if . . ."

2. **ASC 360-10-35-17** _____: "An impairment loss shall be recognized only if . . ."

3. _____ **ASC 360-10-35-17**: "An impairment loss shall be recognized only if . . ."

4. Show two ways that the underlined words in this reference could be stated more clearly.

According to **ASC 360-10-35-17** it states: "An impairment loss shall be recognized only if . . ."

_____ or _____

Now
[YOU]
Try
3.8

Should I Ever Use Footnotes in Professional Memos?

The use of footnotes and endnotes (that is, numerical references leading readers to a "works cited" source at the end of a page or document) should be fairly rare in accounting research memos. That is, you should primarily expect to cite the Codification or other authoritative sources of guidance, and these source references can be included in the body of your memos.

Footnotes or endnotes are appropriate, however, if you are referencing a less-common source of guidance, which requires a lengthier source citation. For example, if you find guidance in an academic paper or in a professional journal, a footnote or endnote citation is appropriate, as the reference must include not only the author's name, but the article name, date published, title of journal, edition number, and page number. Including all of this detail in the body of a memo would bog down your reader.

When Should I Use Quotation Marks?

Any guidance copied directly from the Codification must be enclosed in double quotation marks, *and* you must cite the source of the guidance down to the paragraph-level of detail (e.g., Per **ASC xxx-xx-xx-xx . . .**).

> For example, **ASC 715-30-35-47** (Compensation—Pension) states: "The expected long-term rate of return on plan assets shall reflect the average rate of earnings expected on the funds invested or to be invested to provide for the benefits included in the projected benefit obligation."

Notice the use of double quotation marks to enclose the quote, and notice the full reference to the Codification source.

There is one (and only one) instance in which quotation marks are not required: If you are including a long excerpt—roughly three lines or more—from the Codification, and you *indent the guidance*. Indenting long excerpts (as opposed to integrating the quotation within other text) can also improve the readability of your memo.

EXAMPLE

Consider splitting the Codification reference when indenting guidance. For example, we split this reference between the introduction (715-30) and the excerpt (35-47).

> ASC 715-30 (Compensation—Pension) requires that companies consider future expected returns on investments in selecting an expected return on assets assumption:
>
> **35-47**   The expected long-term rate of return on plan assets shall reflect the average rate of earnings expected on the funds invested or to be invested to provide for the benefits included in the projected benefit obligation. In estimating that rate, appropriate consideration shall be given to the returns being earned by the plan assets in the fund and the rates of return expected to be available for reinvestment . . .
>
> Therefore, an asset return assumption is appropriate if management believes this rate is achievable in the future.

Notice how this example includes both: (1) a reference (**ASC xxx**) down to the paragraph level of detail and (2) guidance that is indented, indicating that it is a direct quote.

When Is It Appropriate to Alter an Excerpt from the Guidance?

It is only appropriate to alter an excerpt from the guidance if (1) in doing so, you do not change the meaning of the guidance, and (2) you clearly tell the reader what you have altered. Use brackets [ ] to identify any words you have changed, or to acknowledge that you have added emphasis to part of a quote.

For example, note the following altered excerpt from **ASC 815-10** (Derivatives and Hedging):

> **15-83.**   "A derivative instrument is a financial instrument or other contract with **all** of the following characteristics . . . " [Emphasis added]

Also note this excerpt from **ASC 842-10** (Leases):

15-3. "A contract is or contains a lease if the contract conveys the right to control the use of identified [PP&E] (an identified asset) for a period of time in exchange for consideration."

In the preceding example, the author omitted the words "property, plant, or equipment" in favor of using the bracketed term "[PP&E]." Additionally, the author added boldface type to the term "all" and acknowledged this change by stating, "[Emphasis added]." As neither change alters the meaning of the guidance, and as both changes were identified with brackets, these changes are appropriate.

When Is It Appropriate to Use Ellipses?

Ellipses, or those three dots in a row (. . .) are used when a writer *omits* some text in a quote or *doesn't quote the full sentence or paragraph*. As you begin writing technical emails and memos, you may find that ellipses are useful in trimming fat; that is, eliminating irrelevant sections from a paragraph may improve the readability of your analysis. While sufficient guidance is critical to a strong issues memo, too much guidance can be burdensome.

EXAMPLE

Here is original guidance from **ASC 405-20** (Extinguishments of Liabilities) describing how a debtor's secondary liability should be recorded as a guarantee.

40-2   If a creditor releases a debtor from primary obligation on the condition that a third party assumes the obligation and that the original debtor becomes secondarily liable, that release extinguishes the original debtor's liability. However, in those circumstances, whether or not explicit consideration was paid for that guarantee, the original debtor becomes a guarantor. As a guarantor, it shall recognize a guarantee obligation in the same manner as would a guarantor that had never been primarily liable to that creditor, with due regard for the likelihood that the third party will carry out its obligations. The guarantee obligation shall be initially measured at fair value, and that amount reduces the gain or increases the loss recognized on extinguishment. See Topic **460** for accounting guidance related to guarantees.

Here's an example of the proper use of an ellipsis to abbreviate a sentence from the preceding text.

40-2   "However . . . , ~~in those circumstances,~~ whether or not explicit consideration was paid for that guarantee, the original debtor becomes a guarantor."

Here's an example illustrating the proper use of an ellipsis when the full paragraph is not being quoted. Here, the ellipsis shows that the paragraph continues on, even beyond this excerpted text.

40-2   "If a creditor releases a debtor from primary obligation on the condition that a third party assumes the obligation and that the original debtor becomes secondarily liable, that release extinguishes the original debtor's liability. However, in those circumstances, whether or not explicit consideration was paid for that guarantee, the original debtor becomes a guarantor . . ."

While ellipses may become a great tool in your toolbox, you must always *check and double check* that the text you are skipping over is not critical to the understanding of a passage, and that using the ellipsis does not change the meaning of the original guidance.

Here's an improper use of an ellipsis. Notice how pertinent guidance has been omitted.

> **40-2** "If a creditor releases a debtor from primary obligation on the condition that a third party assumes the obligation . . . ~~and that the original debtor becomes secondarily liable~~, that release extinguishes the original debtor's liability."

STYLE TIPS FOR PROFESSIONAL COMMUNICATION

LO6 **Communicate** using professional style.

We'll conclude our chapter on communication by discussing a few points on style. Attention to style will improve the professionalism of your work products.

Use Proper Voice in Your Memos

Avoid saying "I" or "we" or "you" in accounting research communications. Technical accounting memos are not about you; they should not be written in the first person.

- For example, do not say: "We found the guidance in **ASC 606**."
- Do not say: "I think" or "We have concluded" in a memo.
- Do not say: "You have asked us for the appropriate accounting treatment . . ." in a memo.

When referring to a company, do not say "they" or "their." Rather, call the company by its name initially, and identify (in parenthesis) any abbreviations you plan to use for the company name thereafter.

- For example, Presto Hospitality ("Presto" or "the Company") shall recognize revenue on a net basis. This is appropriate given the Company's role as agent.

Notice how this example initially introduces Presto Hospitality using its full name, and then uses the parenthetical ("Presto" or "the Company") to show how the company will be described in future references within the memo. Finally, note the following additional examples of proper and improper voice:

- Do say: The Company has evaluated its accounting.
- Do not say: The Company has evaluated their accounting.

Keep Your Language Neutral (Avoid Strong Words)

To improve the professionalism of your writing, keep your language neutral. I once asked students to review a company's accounting election and to comment on whether it was supportable based on guidance from the Codification. A few students described the company's position as "wrong," and one may have even called the company's accounting "ridiculous."

The lesson here: Try to leave your emotions out of technical writing. Keep your language neutral. Here are examples of more appropriate ways to comment on an accounting position. The accounting is

- "Appropriate/not appropriate."
- "Consistent/not consistent with" the guidance.
- "Supported/not supported by" the guidance.

Also, try to avoid "absolutes" in your technical writing. It's better to play it safe and use qualifying words.

- Use the word "generally" rather than "always."
  - Analysts "generally" (not "always") listen to companies' earnings calls for the purpose of understanding more of the qualitative factors behind a company's performance.
- Use the word "could" rather than "will."
  - The company "could" (not "will") have to restate later if it chooses an accounting position that is not supported by the guidance.
- Use the word "specialist" rather than "expert."

As a check of your word choice, reread your work and ask yourself: *Would I be comfortable if a quote from this work appeared in the newspaper?* This same advice is commonly given to CPA firms by their attorneys, according to a retired "Big Four" partner.

> One of the writing conventions that I picked up during my time at the FASB is use of the verbs *states, stated,* or *said* in technical writing. The guidance *states.* The Board members *stated.* My project manager's red pen frequently came out when my draft board minutes included more creative terms such as "argued," "pointed out," or "asserted." In each case, he suggested that I change the word to "stated" or "said." (Board minutes have since changed to focus on decisions reached, as opposed to discussions held.)

TIP | from the Trenches

Get the Grammar Right

Grammatical errors in your writing can undermine the quality of your whole research effort. Before submitting a memo to your supervisor or to a client, carefully reread it for proper grammar, spelling, and clarity. Even an offense as seemingly minor as a misplaced comma can tarnish the polish on an otherwise great paper.

Commas

Following is a brief refresher on commas. If this is a trouble area for you, please review this section carefully.

- Use commas between "independent clauses"—each with a *subject* and a *verb*:
  - *I went* to the store, and *you went* home.
  - Comparative *income statements must* be presented for three years, but comparative *balance sheets must* be presented for two years.
  - Note: Each of these clauses could be a sentence all by itself, so a comma is needed between them.
- Use commas after an *introductory phrase*:
  - *Although the company's earnings were below expectations,* the company's stock price did not change.
  - *If two alternatives are available,* both should be analyzed in your memo.
  - Note: Note that each phrase has its own subject and verb; the introductory phrase also includes a transition (if, although, after, before, etc.). Separate these two phrases with a comma.
- Use commas when you insert a phrase into a sentence that isn't necessary for understanding the sentence.
  - He said, *with an encouraging nod,* that I should read more.
  - Nonauthoritative guidance, *which is available from a number of different sources,* can be useful in supporting authoritative references.
  - Note: If the phrases "with an encouraging nod" or "which is available from a number of different sources" were stricken from these sentences, the sentences would still read

just as clearly. As these phrases are purely descriptive, and not necessary for understanding the sentence, they are set off in commas.

Criteria versus Criterion

Students are frequently uncertain how to form the singular, verus plural, form of the word *criteria*. Here's the deal:

- *Criteria* is plural. There are *five criteria* for evaluating lease classification.
- *Criterion* is singular. The *first criterion* involves whether the lease transfers ownership by the end of the lease term.

Getting Feedback on Your Writing

I still, to this day, cringe when I get feedback on my work. This may be a natural thing to do. But I've also learned to tell myself: "Wait. I can learn from this." And just like that, I go from dreading the feedback to appreciating the learning opportunity it presents.

If your instructor or supervisor takes the time to provide feedback on your writing, understand that they do this because they *believe in your potential to improve*. I can attest that providing detailed feedback to each student takes a ton of time. Take the time to read and learn from any comments you are given.

Consider taking the following steps when getting feedback:

1. Don't panic when it's given to you. Think: *I can learn from this.*
2. Read it closely, and with an open mind. If you don't understand the feedback, ask for clarification.
3. Appreciate the feedback—either silently or by thanking the person who provided it.

As you advance in your career, there may be increasing circumstances where you consider, but then reject, feedback you are given. In many cases, however, you aren't there yet! Be open to learning from others.

Common Instructor Notations

For reference, here are some notations that I commonly use in providing handwritten feedback to my students. Your instructor may (or may not) use similar notations.

¶	Start a new paragraph.
S/, C/, W/	Should, could, or would
S/b, C/b, W/b	Should be, could be, would be
^	Insert
= dbl underline	The first letters should be uppercase.
~~S~~trikethrough	The first letter should be lowercase.
sp	Spelling error
stet	Means: "What you had is fine. Disregard my comment."
ℯ	Delete
w/r/t	with respect to
K	contract

CHAPTER 3 APPENDIX

Sample Accounting Issues Memo

The following Presto Hospitality memo is only partially complete and is provided for example purposes. Additional issues will need to be evaluated in order to fully conclude on the accounting for this arrangement.

Draft—For Discussion Purposes Only

> Use this DRAFT stamp in the header until final contracts have been reviewed.

Memorandum

To: Presto Hospitality Accounting Files

From: Michael Jones, Accounting Policy team

Date: 12/1/20X1

Re: Accounting for concessions agreement with Stadium Co.

> Describe the type of transaction succinctly in the "Re" line.

Facts

Presto Hospitality (Presto) is a public company that is in the process of signing a 10-year concessions agreement with a major league baseball stadium owner (Stadium Co.). The agreement would give Presto the right and obligation to operate all of the stadium's fixed concession stands and portable food and beverage carts, to provide food and beverage service to premium seating areas (including suites), and to have hawkers selling concessions in the aisles of the stadium (Sodas! Peanuts!), collectively, the "Food and Beverage Facilities." The locations of fixed concession stands within the stadium are designated in architectural drawings included within the draft concessions agreement. The draft contract states that Stadium Co., at its option and at its cost (such as the cost to rebuild leasehold improvements), can require Presto to move its locations within the stadium.

The concessions agreement will require Presto to remit 50% of its gross food sales and 52% of its gross alcohol sales to Stadium Co. in exchange for the right to operate at the stadium. Presto will also be required to make an upfront payment of $5 million to Stadium Co., which will be used toward capital improvements, build-outs, and branding of the concession facilities. Throughout the operating period of this agreement, Stadium Co. will have the right to approve all of Presto's proposed menu items, pricing, and choices of suppliers, and Stadium Co. has indicated during negotiations that it plans to actively exercise this approval authority. To be chosen as the concession provider for this stadium, Presto submitted a successful bid and was selected from a group of competing potential concessionaires.

Presto must determine whether this arrangement contains a lease within the scope of ASC 842 (Leases).

> If the transaction is complex or involves multiple parties, include a picture here.

Issues

1. Does the Concessions Agreement involve an *identified asset*?
2. *List additional questions here.*

> Phrase issues in the form of a question.

Analysis—Issue 1: Does the Concessions Agreement involve an *identified asset*?

FASB Accounting Standards Codification (ASC) 842-10 (Leases) provides the following scope guidance for determining whether an arrangement is or contains a lease:

> **15-3** A contract is or contains a lease if the contract conveys the right to control the use of identified property, plant, or equipment (an identified asset) for a period of time in exchange for consideration…

Continued

Continued from previous page

ASC 842-10 states the following with respect to determining whether a contract involves an *identified asset:*

> **15-9** An asset typically is identified by being explicitly specified in a contract. However, an asset also can be identified by being implicitly specified at the time that the asset is made available for use by the customer.

The baseball stadium (an asset) is explicitly specified in the contract. However, Presto only has the right to use specified portions of the stadium. Accordingly, two challenges that arise in applying the concept of *identified asset* to this agreement include evaluating 1) when a *portion of an asset* is an identified asset and 2) whether the supplier has a *substantive right to substitute* the asset. We will evaluate each of these conditions next.

Consider using italicized subheaders to help organize discussion points within your memo.

Portion of an Asset

Par. 15-16 provides the following guidance regarding whether a portion of an asset is an identified asset:

> > > > Portions of Assets
>
> **15-16** A capacity portion of an asset is an identified asset if it is **physically distinct** (for example, a floor of a building or a segment of a pipeline that connects a single customer to the larger pipeline). A capacity or other portion of an asset that is not physically distinct (for example, a capacity portion of a fiber optic cable) is not an identified asset, unless it represents substantially all of the capacity of the asset and thereby provides the customer with the right to obtain substantially all of the economic benefits from use of the asset. [Emphasis added]

As the Food and Beverage Facilities represent a portion of a broader asset (the Stadium), these facilities are only considered an *identified asset* if they are *physically distinct.*

PwC's *Leases* guide book (2018) offers the following additional, interpretive guidance for assessing whether a portion of an asset is physically distinct:

Present non-authoritative sources in guidance sandwiches following consideration of authoritative guidance.

> An identified asset must be physically distinct. A physically distinct asset may be an entire asset or a portion of an asset. For example, a building is generally considered physically distinct, but one floor within the building may also be considered physically distinct if it can be used independent of the other floors (e.g., point of ingress or egress, access to lavatories, etc.). (Sec. 2.3.1.3)

In this arrangement, certain of the Food and Beverage Facilities (specifically, fixed concession stands) are specified on architectural drawings and are thus physically distinct. Additionally, the right to serve food and beverages in premium seating areas, including suites, involves physically distinct spaces. These concession stands and premium areas can be used independently from one another. Therefore, these spaces are all considered *physically distinct.*

By contrast, other rights in the contract, such as the right to operate portables and the right to have food and beverage hawkers operating throughout the stadium, do not involve physically distinct portions of an asset. The location of the portable carts is not specified, and therefore any location within the stadium could be used to locate the carts. Per par. 15-16, if a portion of an asset is not physically distinct, it "is not an identified asset, unless it represents substantially all of the capacity of the asset…". This condition is not present, as use of the portables and rights of the hawkers within the broader Stadium do not represent "substantially all" of the Stadium's capacity. Therefore, these rights do not involve identified assets.

Substantive Right to Substitute

An additional requirement for a contract to include an *identified asset* is that the supplier cannot have the "substantive right to substitute" the asset during the period of use. This requirement is described in par. 15-10 as follows:

Continued from previous page

15-10 Even if an asset is specified, a customer does not have the right to use an identified asset if the supplier has the substantive right to substitute the asset throughout the period of use. A supplier's right to substitute an asset is substantive only if **both** of the following conditions exist:

a. The supplier has the practical ability to substitute alternative assets throughout the period of use (for example, the customer cannot prevent the supplier from substituting an asset, and alternative assets are readily available to the supplier or could be sourced by the supplier within a reasonable period of time).

b. The supplier would benefit economically from the exercise of its right to substitute the asset (that is, the economic benefits associated with substituting the asset are expected to exceed the costs associated with substituting the asset). [Emphasis added]

According to the concessions agreement, Stadium Co. can require Presto to relocate its facilities within the stadium. Therefore, it is necessary to evaluate whether this substitution right is "substantive" by evaluating the conditions in par. 15-10(a) and (b).

Practical Ability to Substitute (par. 15-10a): Stadium Co. has the practical ability to substitute alternative assets throughout the period of use, as it has the stated right per the contract to make changes to the specified facilities. Furthermore, alternate locations within the Stadium are available to Stadium Co. that could be used to substitute Presto's designated spaces in the Stadium. Therefore, par. 15-10(a) is met for all concession spaces in the contract.

Economically would benefit from substitution (par. 15-10b): It is unclear whether the economic benefits to Stadium Co. associated with substituting the designated food and beverage spaces would be expected to exceed the costs associated with substituting these spaces. Stadium Co. would presumably incur significant relocation costs if it were to require Presto to change the location of a fixed concession stand in the Stadium, given the kitchen and other equipment involved in such a relocation effort. On the other hand, food and beverage kiosks (portables) could easily be moved without significant cost.

To assist in our evaluation of this "economic benefit" condition, we considered the following implementation guidance from ASC 842-10 involving a portable concession stand. While we already concluded that the spaces on which portables will be located are not physically distinct portions of assets, we will evaluate this example for the avoidance of doubt.

> > > Example 2—Concession Space

55-52 A coffee company (Customer) enters into a contract with an airport operator (Supplier) to use a space in the airport to sell its goods for a three-year period. The contract states the amount of space and that the space may be located at any one of several boarding areas within the airport. Supplier has the right to change the location of the space allocated to Customer at any time during the period of use. There are minimal costs to Supplier associated with changing the space for the Customer: Customer uses a kiosk (that it owns) that can be moved easily to sell its goods. There are many areas in the airport that are available and that would meet the specifications for the space in the contract.

Indent excerpts to improve the readability of your memo.

55-53 The contract does not contain a lease.

55-54 Although the amount of space Customer uses is specified in the contract, there is no identified asset. Customer controls its owned kiosk. However, the contract is for space in the airport, and this space can change at the discretion of Supplier. Supplier has the substantive right to substitute the space Customer uses because:

a. Supplier has the practical ability to change the space used by Customer throughout the period of use. There are many areas in the airport that meet the specifications for the space in the contract, and Supplier has the right to change the location of the space to other space that meets the specifications at any time without Customer's approval.

b. Supplier would benefit economically from substituting the space. There would be minimal cost associated with changing the space used by Customer because the kiosk can be moved easily. Supplier benefits from substituting the space in the airport because substitution allows Supplier to make the most effective use of the space at boarding areas in the airport to meet changing circumstances.

Continued

Continued from previous page

This par. 55-52 example involves an airport kiosk whose location can be easily changed. This is analogous to the portables involved in Presto's agreement, which can be easily moved. Consistent with this example, Stadium Co.'s substitution right is substantive with respect to portable concession spaces.

However, with respect to more "fixed" locations, such as concession stands with kitchen equipment, the guidance offers an example illustrating that moving such spaces could impose economic cost to the supplier (Stadium Co.):

> **55-63** Customer enters into a contract with property owner (Supplier) to use Retail Unit A for a five-year period. Retail Unit A is part of a larger retail space with many retail units.

> **55-64** Customer is granted the right to use Retail Unit A. Supplier can require Customer to relocate to another retail unit. In that case, Supplier is required to provide Customer with a retail unit of similar quality and specifications to Retail Unit A and to pay for Customer's relocation costs. Supplier would benefit economically from relocating Customer only if a major new tenant were to decide to occupy a large amount of retail space at a rate sufficiently favorable to cover the costs of relocating Customer and other tenants in the retail space that the new tenant will occupy. However, although it is possible that those circumstances will arise, at inception of the contract, it is not likely that those circumstances will arise. For example, whether a major new tenant will decide to lease a large amount of retail space at a rate that would be sufficiently favorable to cover the costs of relocating Customer is highly susceptible to factors outside Supplier's influence.

> . . . **55-69** Retail Unit A is an identified asset. It is explicitly specified in the contract. Supplier has the practical ability to substitute the retail unit, but could benefit economically from substitution only in specific circumstances. Supplier's substitution right is not substantive because, at inception of the contract, those circumstances are not considered likely to arise.

In this example, it is considered unlikely at inception of an arrangement that the supplier would move a customer using "Retail Unit A." Despite the availability of other retail units that could be substituted for Retail Unit A, the supplier's costs in moving the customer would not be expected to exceed the benefits. Therefore, the supplier's substitution right is not considered *substantive*. Consistent with this example, in Presto's arrangement, fixed concession stands and premium areas would be costly to move and therefore would not likely be subject to substitution. Per discussions with Presto management, based on its prior experiences with similar contracts, the food and beverage locations within the stadium are generally unlikely to be changed by the stadium owner.

Conclusion—Issue 1: Identified Asset

The Food and Beverage Facilities are a portion of an asset, and thus these spaces are considered "identified assets" if they are physically distinct and not subject to substantive substitution rights. We have concluded the following:

- Fixed concession stands, suites, and premium areas are physically distinct and are not subject to a substantive substitution right (given that relocation would be costly and thus unlikely). These locations are considered identified assets.
- With respect to the right for hawkers to operate in the stadium, the hawkers are not limited to a defined space (i.e., the space is not physically distinct), and thus this right does not involve an identified asset.
- With respect to portables, the locations are not physically distinct, *and* Stadium Co. has a substantive right of substitution. Thus, portables are not considered *identified assets.*

Therefore, the identified assets in this arrangement are 1) fixed concession stands and 2) premium seating areas and suites.

Given that this is not a complete memo, the "Financial Statement and Disclosure Impacts" section of the memo has been omitted.

CHAPTER SUMMARY

Effective documentation serves several functions for the company and its auditor. Not only does the process of creating documentation allow the accountant to think critically about the issues at hand, but a complete set of documentation serves as support for key judgments, a valuable historical reference, and—in the case of auditors—evidence of a robust evaluation of client positions.

This chapter introduced a standard format for preparing accounting issues memoranda and professional emails. The chapter also provided style tips for professional communication, including how to cite from the FASB Codification, use neutral language, and use professional voice. Commit these tips to memory, as they will serve you well in your professional career.

REVIEW QUESTIONS

1. Cite two reasons why documentation is a critical part of performing accounting research.
2. Explain how creating clear documentation might provide some protection against hindsight bias.
3. Contrast the circumstances in which an email should be used to communicate research, versus circumstances in which a memo may be warranted.
4. Name three of the tips provided for drafting effective emails.
5. The chapter notes that email communications should be kept fairly brief. In light of this, is it appropriate to include guidance excerpts in an email? Explain.
6. Name the sections included in the standard memo format introduced in this chapter.
7. Explain what is meant by the statement that a memo should be a one-stop shop.
8. How much detail should be included in the Facts section of an issues memo?
9. Should your issues list always be organized around the case study questions, as given to you? Explain.
10. Complete the following sentence. Issues should be phrased in the form of _____.
11. What is the goal of the Analysis section of the memo? Explain.
12. When alternative accounting methods are available, why is it essential for a researcher to identify these possible alternatives in his or her documentation?
13. In what circumstances might subheaders be useful to help organize your analysis?
14. Explain why researchers should include actual excerpts from the guidance in accounting memoranda, rather than paraphrases of guidance (in the researcher's own words).
15. Which section of an accounting issues memorandum is often enhanced by a picture (or diagram) of the transaction?
16. Is it acceptable to document other sources considered, such as nonauthoritative sources, in a memo? Explain.
17. What is meant by the advice: Don't *jump* to conclusions!
18. What does the term "guidance sandwiches" mean? Where would you find these in an accounting issues memorandum?
19. Should new arguments or guidance references be introduced in the Conclusion section of a memo? Explain.
20. Why is a Conclusion section necessary in an issues memo?
21. What is the role of journal entries in an accounting issues memo? Where should these be discussed?
22. What are three things you should check for when reviewing your writing?
23. How should a researcher refer to guidance from the Codification, the first time it is cited in a memo?
24. Which of the following Codification references is stronger? Explain.
    - *Per* ASC xxx: "Quote"
    - ASC xxx *asks readers to* . . . "Quote"
25. Describe what "voice" should be used in accounting research communications. (Feel free to respond by describing what voices "should not" be used.)
26. Explain what it means for the language in an accounting memorandum to be "neutral."

EXERCISES

1. For each of the following pieces of information, state whether it should be included in, or excluded from, the Facts section of an issues memo, assuming that the objective of the issues memo is to evaluate the accounting by a company for a repurchase of its own stock. Briefly explain your reasoning.

    a. The fact that the issuer is a public company.

    b. The market value of the company's stock on the date the program commences.

    c. The anticipated size of the repurchase program, in dollars.

    d. The period over which the repurchase program is expected to occur.

    e. Background on the company and its primary sources of revenue.

    f. The fact that the company entered into a similar transaction several years ago.

    g. The name of the investment bank that will facilitate and manage the repurchase program.

2. As the Presto Hospitality memo in this chapter illustrates, accounting issues are not always straightforward. The following questions are intended to highlight some of the many judgments and alternatives present in that memo. Considering that memo, respond to the following. Use the Presto Hospitality memo, and your own thinking, to respond. (Codification research is not necessary for this exercise.)

    a. Why is it important for Presto to determine whether the concessions agreement is a lease? What impacts could this conclusion have on Presto's accounting?

    b. Describe the steps involved in performing the analysis of which concession locations/rights are considered *identified assets*.

    c. What would have happened if Presto had concluded that the arrangement does not involve *identified assets*? What analysis would have been performed next?

    d. What value did the airport kiosk implementation guidance example contribute to Presto's evaluation of its *identified assets*?

    e. What value did the Retail Unit A implementation guidance example contribute to Presto's evaluation of its *identified assets*?

    f. The Conclusion section laid out not only the conclusion for each concession right/location, but also the rationale. Summarize the rationale described for each conclusion reached.

3. Draw a picture illustrating the following fact pattern:

    Truck Co., a wholly owned subsidiary of Auto Corp., is selling its light-duty truck plant to Company B for $10 million. Company B has taken out a loan for $8 million from Sub Bank in anticipation of the exchange. Sub Bank is a wholly owned subsidiary of Parent Bank.

4. Draw a picture illustrating the following fact pattern involving an *interest rate swap:*

    Company C has issued bonds that pay LIBOR (a floating rate) to investors (in exchange for cash). Company D has issued bonds with a fixed 6% rate to investors (in exchange for cash), with interest payable semiannually. Company C and Company D enter into an interest rate swap. In this swap, Company C will pay a fixed 6% rate to Bank (a financial intermediary); in turn, Bank passes this payment on to Company D. Company D will pay LIBOR to Bank, which in turn passes this payment on to Company C. (Through this derivative transaction, Company C has essentially converted its payment obligation from a floating to a fixed rate; Company D has converted its obligation from fixed to floating).

    (*Hint:* To begin this picture, draw four boxes in a row horizontally, to depict, respectively, Investors, Company C, Company D, Investors. There should be lines between each company and its investors depicting the consideration they exchange. Above this horizontal row, draw one box for Bank.)

5. a. Draw a picture illustrating the following fact pattern involving *trust-preferred securities*:

    Bank S sets up a trust (a subsidiary entity) and owns 100% of the common stock in the trust. That trust issues preferred securities to investors (in exchange for cash), and the investors earn periodic fixed dividend payments on their preferred shares. Using the funds from the sale of preferred stock, the trust purchases junior subordinated debt from Bank S, and this debt pays periodic fixed interest payments equal to the dividend payments made by the trust. The trust has a call option, allowing it to call back the preferred shares from investors at its option. Additionally, Bank S has a call option, allowing it to call back its debt from the trust at its option. Bank S guarantees to the trust's investors that the trust will use its available cash to make interest payments.

    b. Next, imagine that you are writing an issues memo documenting this arrangement from Bank S's perspective. What are four researchable questions that you might list in the Issues section of the memo?

6. *a.* Briefly, describe whether your base-level understanding of interest rate swaps and trust-preferred securities has improved after completing exercises 4–5 above. Explain.

   b. Now, describe one other circumstance in which drawing a picture could be useful in performing or communicating accounting research.

7. Locate Codification guidance describing how inventory should initially be measured, and present the excerpt in a *guidance sandwich*. Assume you are answering the question: Should inventory be measured initially at its market value or at cost?

8. Read the following issue. Next, add an ellipsis to par. 15-2 to reflect the removal of any guidance not considered relevant to this issue.

   Issue: Presto Hospitality is researching the interaction between ASC 842 (Leases) and ASC 606 (Revenue). Presto wants to know whether it must evaluate ASC 606 for any contracts that it concludes are within the scope of leasing guidance. Presto reviews the following scope guidance in ASC 606-10:

   15-2 An entity shall apply the guidance in this Topic to all contracts with customers, except the following:
   a. Lease contracts within the scope of Topic 842, Leases.
   b. Contracts within the scope of Topic 944, Financial Services—Insurance.
   c. Financial instruments and other contractual rights or obligations within the scope of the following Topics:
   1. Topic 310, Receivables
   2. Topic 320, Investments—Debt and Equity Securities
   2a. Topic 321, Investments—Equity Securities
   3. Topic 323, Investments—Equity Method and Joint Ventures
   4. Topic 325, Investments—Other
   5. Topic 405, Liabilities
   6. Topic 470, Debt
   7. Topic 815, Derivatives and Hedging
   8. Topic 825, Financial Instruments
   9. Topic 860, Transfers and Servicing.
   d. Guarantees (other than product or service warranties) within the scope of Topic 460, Guarantees.
   e. Nonmonetary exchanges between entities in the same line of business to facilitate sales to customers or potential customers. For example, this Topic would not apply to a contract between two oil companies that agree to an exchange of oil to fulfill demand from their customers in different specified locations on a timely basis. Topic 845 on nonmonetary transactions may apply to nonmonetary exchanges that are not within the scope of this Topic.

9. Correct any errors in the following paragraph, or fix any areas where the professionalism of the writing could be improved. Consider proper voice, language, and punctuation. You do not need to use the Codification to complete this exercise.

   In my opinion Beta Corp's ("their") accounting is wrong because they are applying revenue recognition guidance to a lease contract, even though lease transactions are exempted from Code 606. Code Section 606-15-2 says that "a. Lease contracts within the scope of Topic 842, Leases" are not subject to revenue recognition guidance.

10. Change the following sentences to active voice.
    a. The incorrect accounting applied by the company resulted in a restatement.
    b. A new standard was issued by the FASB that will result in changes to long-duration insurance contracts.

11. Add commas to the following sentences, and for each sentence briefly justify why the commas were needed.
    a. Although Apple's sales remained stagnant in Q2 its stock price rose.
    b. Jones Company which is based in India is privately held.
    c. We need to audit the company's accounts receivable accounts payable and cash accounts.
    d. Presto will make an upfront payment and Stadium Co. will use the funds toward capital improvements.

12. Replace the following weak Codification references with stronger language.
    a. I found the following guidance in ASC 360-10-35-3, "Depreciation expense in financial statements for an asset shall be determined based on the asset's useful life."
    b. Per GASB Statement No. 51, ". . . all intangible assets not specifically excluded by its scope provisions be classified as capital assets." (Summary page).
    c. In the Codification, ASC 450-20-25-2 says that "An estimated loss from a loss contingency shall be accrued by a charge to income if both . . ."

[Hint: This letter (b) example starts with a *strong* reference, but the reference doesn't flow with the rest of the quote. Find a way to fix this.]

13. Introduce the following guidance using a strong reference, then indent the guidance following your introduction. Split the guidance reference (topic-subtopic), (section-paragraph) in a manner similar to the example shown on p. 96.

> ASC 210-10-45-13 (Balance Sheet)
>
> Asset valuation allowances for losses such as those on receivables and investments shall be deducted from the assets or groups of assets to which the allowances relate.

14. In the following excerpt, explain why *brackets* [ ] are present (e.g., what are the two functions of the brackets in this example?). Also, explain why it's necessary for the researcher to show any changes to quoted text in brackets.

> Per ASC 842-10-15-3: "A contract is or contains a lease if the contract conveys the **right to control** the use of identified [PP&E] (an identified asset) for a period of time in exchange for consideration." [Emphasis added]

CASE STUDY QUESTIONS

3.1   **Presto Hospitality—Lease Scope** In Case Study 2.5, you researched whether Presto has the right to substantially all economic benefits from use of the identified assets. Now, research whether Presto has the **right to direct** use of the identified assets. In doing so, assume that the stadium owner has the right, per contract, to require Presto to change the "concept" offered at the concession stands at its option. For example, Stadium Owner could require that a hot dog stand be changed out for a pizza concept. However, assume, in practice, that the stadium owner may only exercise this authority once per year, perhaps for one concession stand out of the several stands run by Presto. Also, assume that Presto can recommend pricing to the Stadium Owner, but ultimate approval authority rests with the Stadium Owner.

   As necessary, identify additional questions you might ask—or facts you might gather—in order to fully research this question.

   Next, benchmark against peer disclosures: Do other companies with similar activities report these contracts as leases?

3.2   **Presto Hospitality—Lease Scope** Describe the decisions in the Presto Hospitality arrangement that are *predetermined* versus decisions that remain to be made throughout the contract term. These are the decisions that comprise right to direct.

3.3   **Presto Hospitality—Lease Scope**
   a. Evaluate how Presto's lease scope assessment would be impacted if the arrangement were priced differently. For example, would you conclude that the arrangement is a lease if the contract is called a Management Agreement and the arrangement is priced such that Presto earns a fixed management fee of $100,000 per year? Assume in that case that all operating profit or loss would be borne by Stadium Owner.
   b. What if Presto earns a fixed fee of $85,000 per year + 1% of gross sales + 10% of profits? How does this pricing affect your analysis of lease scope?

3.4   **Presto Hospitality—Lease Scope** A colleague in your accounting policy group came across guidance in Deloitte's lease accounting Roadmap publication that describes a concept of functional independence. Your colleague believes Presto could make the case that its concession stands are not "functionally independent" of the stadium, noting for example that Presto cannot independently market its stands to customers unless those customers have a ticket to enter the stadium. Evaluate the strength of this argument, and describe the implications of taking this position on Presto's accounting.

3.5   **Presto Hospitality—Revenue Recognition** Assume Presto concludes that its concession agreement with Stadium Co. is not a lease. In that case, apply the five-step revenue process in ASC 606 to this arrangement. Assume you are evaluating appropriate revenue recognition for the contract and for individual transactions that will arise within the scope of the contract (for example, a sale of a hot dog to a customer in the stadium). Assume a hot dog retails for $6, of which Presto retains 50%.

3.6   **Baseball Suites—Lease Evaluation** The New York Yankees offer multiyear luxury suite licenses to customers, including 3-, 5-, and 10-year licenses. Customers who sign these license agreements have the right to use a specified suite in the stadium (say, suite no. 25) for the dates specified in the license agreement. Alternatively, customers with a more limited interest or budget can sign up for a partial season (a 20- or 41-game plan) where the customer can specify which games it wishes to view from the suite. While the customer is enjoying the suite, a third-party conces-sionaire (similar to Presto's role) will provide premium food and beverage service to guests in the suite. Evaluate—is a suite license a lease? Assume a customer signs a 20-game license for specified games to occur within a single Major League Baseball season.

Sales Commissions, Writing an Email Assume the New York Yankees pay its sales staff a 2% sales commission on each luxury suite license contract signed (such as by a corporate customer). Research whether this commission payment should be reported as an asset or an expense by the New York Yankees. Craft your response in the form of an email, and assume you're responding to a question asked to you by the accounting manager for the Yankees.

3.7

Why Documentation Matters A company is evaluating a lease to determine whether it should be classified as a finance or operating lease and concludes that it should be reported as a finance lease. However, company accountants realize that a similar lease contract, executed just two years ago, has been accounted for as an operating lease. The company is unable to locate documentation explaining the rationale for the earlier lease's operating classification. Think through this issue. What should the company do? What lessons can the company learn from this?

3.8

Writing an Analysis—Derivatives *Facts*: You are a corporate accountant for Theta, Inc. Today's date is 12/31/20X5. You've been asked to review a contract in which Theta agrees to purchase 200 shares of IBM stock from Delta (seller) in 1 year (on 12/31/20x6), for $140 per share. Said another way, Theta has entered into a forward contract for the purchase of stock.

3.9

Required: Act as though you are writing just the Analysis section of an issues memo, and research the following ques-tion: Does Theta's contract with Delta meet the definition of a derivative? In your response, include applicable excerpts and guidance sandwiches that relate the guidance to this fact pattern.

In your research, you need only consider the following paragraphs from the guidance:
> ASC 815-10-05-4
> ASC 815-10-10-1
> ASC 815-10-15-83, 15-88, 15-92, 15-96
> ASC 815-10-15-119 and 120

In your analysis, include only those paragraphs that are most responsive to this issue. Assume that no scope excep-tions apply.

Drafting an Email, Earnings per Share Your audit team is reviewing the third quarter financial statements of Smirks, Inc., a publicly traded company. The audit manager, Jason, thinks the client may have omitted an important item and has asked you to research whether interim financial statements are required to include earnings per share amounts. Prepare an email responding to Jason's question. Comment on any other potential ramifications of Smirks, Inc.'s omission that come to mind, which you can offer to research.

3.10

Writing a Short Issues Memo—Inventory Valuation You have been asked to draft a brief issues memo ("to the files") analyzing the following issue.

3.11

> Charles Corp. has leased a mine from which it recently extracted 2,000 kilograms of bauxite (a min-eral used in producing aluminum). Charles Corp. plans to sell the bauxite to aluminum manufacturers. Charles Corp. is analyzing whether its bauxite inventory can be carried at its selling price per ASC 330-10-35-16(b). Assume that quoted market prices are generally available for bauxite, and that the market for bauxite is active.

Using the standard memo format, analyze whether all necessary conditions are met for the accounting treatment proposed. If assumptions are needed to fully evaluate the guidance, identify those assumptions in your analysis. For this particular memo, you are not required to present alternative treatments; assume for this issue that you have solely been asked to document whether the conditions in ASC 330-10-35-16(b) are met.

Index

Notes

Notes

Notes

Notes

Notes

Notes

Notes